The Moynihan Report

**THE NEGRO FAMILY—
THE CASE FOR NATIONAL ACTION**

The Moynihan Report

THE NEGRO FAMILY—
THE CASE FOR NATIONAL ACTION

OFFICE OF POLICY PLANNING AND RESEARCH
OF U.S. DEPARTMENT OF LABOR

DANIEL MOYNIHAN

COSIMOREPORTS

NEW YORK

The Moynihan Report:—The Negro Family—The Case for National Action
Current edition published by Cosimo Classics in 2018.
Originally published March 1965.

ISBN: 978-1-94593-429-2

This edition is a classic text and may be considered rare. As such, it is possible that some of the text might be blurred or of reduced print quality. Thank you for your under-standing and we wish you a pleasant reading experience.

Cosimo aims to publish books that inspire, inform, and engage readers worldwide. We use innovative print-on-demand technology that enables books to be printed based on specific customer needs. This approach eliminates an artificial scarcity of publications and allows us to distribute books in the most efficient and environmentally sustainable manner. Cosimo also works with printers and paper manufacturers who practice and encourage sustainable forest management, using paper that has been certified by the FSC, SFI, and PEFC whenever possible.

Ordering Information:
Cosimo publications are available at online bookstores. They may also be purchased for educational, business, or promotional use:
Bulk orders: Special discounts are available on bulk orders for reading groups, organizations, businesses, and others.
Custom-label orders: We offer selected books with your customized cover or logo of choice.

For more information, contact www.cosimobooks.com.

I have endeavoured to prove that the invaluable principle of individual freedom—which, from the Normal Conquest downward, fired the most noble-minded of our ancestors to rebel against the tyranny of those who won, or inherited, the rights of the conquest—is in imminent danger of being lost to us, at the very hour of its consummation.

—from the Preface

Two hundred years ago, in 1765, nine assembled colonies first joined together to demand freedom from arbitrary power.

For the first century we struggled to hold together the first continental union of democracy in the history of man. One hundred years ago, in 1865, following a terrible test of blood and fire, the compact of union was finally sealed.

For a second century we labored to establish a unity of purpose and interest among the many groups which make up the American community.

That struggle has often brought pain and violence. It is not yet over.

State of the Union Message of President Lyndon B. Johnson, January 4, 1965.

The United States is approaching a new crisis in race relations.

In the decade that began with the school desegregation decision of the Supreme Court, and ended with the passage of the Civil Rights Act of 1964, the demand of Negro Americans for full recognition of their civil rights was finally met.

The effort, no matter how savage and brutal, of some State and local governments to thwart the exercise of those rights is doomed. The nation will not put up with it—least of all the Negroes. The present moment will pass. In the meantime, a new period is beginning.

In this new period the expectations of the Negro Americans will go beyond civil rights. Being Americans, they will now expect that in the near future equal opportunities for them as a group will produce roughly equal results, as compared with other groups. This is not going to happen. Nor will it happen for generations to come unless a new and special effort is made.

There are two reasons. First, the racist virus in the American blood stream still afflicts us: Negroes will encounter serious personal prejudice for at least another generation. Second, three centuries of sometimes unimaginable mistreatment have taken their toll on the Negro people. The harsh fact is that as a group, at the present time, in terms of ability to win out in the competitions of American life, they are not equal to most of those groups with which they will be competing. Individually, Negro Americans reach the highest peaks of achievement. But collectively, in the spectrum of American ethnic and religious and regional groups, where some get plenty and some get none, where some send eighty percent of their children to college and others pull them out of school at the 8th grade, Negroes are among the weakest.

The most difficult fact for white Americans to understand is that in these terms the circumstances of the Negro American community in recent years has probably been getting *worse, not better.*

Indices of dollars of income, standards of living, and years of education deceive. The gap between the Negro and most other groups in American society is widening.

The fundamental problem, in which this is most clearly the case, is that of family structure. The evidence—not final, but powerfully persuasive—is that the Negro family in the urban ghettos is crumbling. A middle-class group has managed to save itself, but for vast numbers of the unskilled, poorly educated city working class the fabric of conventional social relationships has all but disintegrated. There are indications that the situation may have been arrested in the past few years, but the general post-war trend is unmistakable. So long as this situation persists, the cycle of poverty and disadvantage will continue to repeat itself.

The thesis of this paper is that these events, in combination, confront the nation with a new kind of problem. Measures that have worked in the past, or would work for most groups in the present, will not work here. A national effort is required that will give a unity of purpose to the many activities of the Federal government in this area, directed to a new kind of national goal: the establishment of a stable Negro family structure.

This would be a new departure for Federal policy. And a difficult one. But it almost certainly offers the only possibility of resolving in our time what is, after all, the nation's oldest, and most intransigent, and now its most dangerous social problem. What Gunnar Myrdal said in *An American Dilemma* remains true today: *"America is free to choose whether the Negro shall remain her liability or become her opportunity."*

TABLE OF CONTENTS

Page

Chapter   I – The Negro American Revolution........................   1

                  The End of the Beginning...........................   1

                  The Demand for Equality   2

                  The Prospect for Equality.........................   4

Chapter   II– The Negro American Family   5

                  Nearly a Quarter of Urban Negro Marriages are Dissolved   6

                  Nearly One-Quarter of Negro Births are Now Illegitimate.....   8

                  Almost One-Fourth of Negro Families are Headed by Females .   9

                  The Breakdown of the Negro Family Has Led to a Startling
Increase in Welfare Dependency..................   12

Chapter III – The Roots of the Problem   15

                  Slavery....................................   15

                  The Reconstruction...........................   16

                  Urbanization   17

                  Unemployment and Poverty   19

                  The Wage System   21

                  The Dimensions Grow   25

Chapter IV – The Tangle of Pathology   29

                  Matriarchy...............................   30

                  The Failure of Youth   34

                  Delinquency and Crime   38

                  The Armed Forces   40

                  Alienation...............................   43

Chapter V – The Case For National Action   47

Footnote References............................   51

Appendix Tables   55

Chapter I

The Negro American Revolution

The Negro American revolution is rightly regarded as the m o s t important domestic event of the postwar period in the United States.

Nothing like it has occurred since the upheavals of the 1930's which led to the organization of the great industrial trade unions, and which in turn profoundly altered both the economy and the political scene. There have been few other events in our history—the American Revolution itself, the surge of Jacksonian Democracy in the 1830's, the Abolitionist movement, and the Populist movement of the late 19th century—comparable to the current Negro movement.

There has been none more important. The Negro American revolution holds forth the prospect that the American Republic, which at birth was f l a w e d by the institution of Negro slavery, and which throughout its history has been marred by the unequal treatment of Negro citizens, will at last redeem the full promise of the Declaration of Independence.

Although the Negro leadership has conducted itself with the strictest propriety, acting always and only as American citizens asserting their rights within the framework of the American political system, it is no less clear that the movement has profound international implications.

It was in no way a matter of chance that the nonviolent tactics and philosophy of the movement, as it began in the South, were consciously adapted from the techniques by which the Congress Party undertook to free the Indian nation from British colonial rule. It was not a matter of chance that the Negro movement caught fire in America at just that

moment when the nations of Africa were gaining their freedom. Nor is it merely incidental that the world should have fastened its attention on events in the United States at a time when the possibility that the nations of the world will divide along color lines seems suddenly not only possible, but even imminent.

(Such racist views have made progress within the Negro American community itself—which can hardly be expected to be immune to a virus that is endemic in the white community. The Black Muslim doctrines, based on total alienation from the white world, exert a powerful influence. On the far left, the attraction of Chinese Communism can no longer be ignored.)

It is clear that what happens in America is being taken as a sign of what can, or must, happen in the world at large. The course of world events will be profoundly affected by the success or failure of the Negro American revolution in seeking the peaceful assimilation of the races in the United States. The award of the Nobel Peace Prize to Dr. Martin Luther King was as much an expression of the hope for the future, as it was recognition for past achievement.

It is no less clear that carrying this revolution forward to a successful conclusion is a first priority confronting the Great Society.

The End of the Beginning

The major e v e n t s of the onset of the Negro revolution are now behind us.

The *political events* were three: First, the Negroes themselves organized as a mass movement. Their organizations have been in some ways better disciplined and better led than any in our history. They have established an unprecedented alliance with religious groups throughout the nation and have maintained close ties with both political parties and with most segments of the trade union movement. Second, the Kennedy-Johnson Administration committed the Federal government to the cause of Negro equality. This had never happened before. Third, the 1964 Presidential election was practically a referendum on this commitment: if these were terms made by the opposition, they were in effect accepted by the President.

The overwhelming victory of President Johnson must be taken as emphatic popular endorsement of the unmistakable, and openly avowed course which the Federal government has pursued under his leadership.

The *administrative events* were threefold as well: First, beginning with the establishment of the President's Committee on Equal Employment Opportunity and on to the enactment of the Manpower Development and Training Act of 1962, the Federal government has launched a major national effort to redress the profound imbalance between the economic position of the Negro citizens and the rest of the nation that derives primarily from their unequal position in the labor market. Second, the Economic Opportunity Act of 1964 began a major national effort to abolish poverty, a condition in which almost half of Negro families are living. Third, the Civil Rights Act of 1964 marked the end of the era of legal and formal discrimination against Negroes and created important new machinery for combating covert discrimination and unequal treatment. (The Act does not guarantee an end to harassment in matters such as voter registration, but does make it more or less incumbent upon government to take further steps to thwart such efforts when they do occur.)

The *legal events* were no less specific. Beginning with *Brown* v. *Board of Education* in 1954, through the decade that culminated

in the recent decisions upholding Title II of the Civil Rights Act, the Federal judiciary, led by the Supreme Court, has used every opportunity to combat unequal treatment of Negro citizens. It may be put as a general proposition that the laws of the United States now look upon any such treatment as obnoxious, and that the courts will strike it down wherever it appears.

The Demand for Equality

With these events behind us, the nation now faces a different set of challenges, which may prove more difficult to meet, if only because they cannot be cast as concrete propositions of right and wrong.

The fundamental problem here is that the Negro revolution, like the industrial upheaval of the 1930's, is a movement for equality as well as for liberty.

Liberty and Equality are the twin ideals of American democracy. But they are not the same thing. Nor, most importantly, are they equally attractive to all groups at any given time; nor yet are they always compatible, one with the other.

Many persons who would gladly die for liberty are appalled by equality. Many who are devoted to equality are puzzled and even troubled by liberty. Much of the political history of the American nation can be seen as a competition between these two ideals, as for example, the unending troubles between capital and labor.

By and large, liberty has been the ideal with the higher social prestige in America. It has been the middle class aspiration, par excellence. (Note the assertions of the conservative right that ours is a republic, not a democracy.) Equality, on the other hand, has enjoyed tolerance more than acceptance. Yet it has roots deep in Western civilization and "is at least coeval with, if not prior to, liberty in the history of Western political thought."[1]

American democracy has not always been successful in maintaining a balance between these two ideals, and notably so where the Negro American is concerned. "Lincoln freed the slaves," but they were given liberty, not equality. It was therefore possible in the century that followed to deprive their descendants of much of their liberty as well.

The ideal of equality does not ordain that all persons end up, as well as start out equal. In traditional terms, as put by Faulkner, "there is no such thing as equality *per se,* but only equality *to*: equal right and opportunity to make the best one can of one's life within one's capability, without fear of injustice or oppression or threat of violence."[2] But the evolution of American politics, with the distinct persistence of ethnic and religious groups, has added a profoundly significant new dimension to that egalitarian ideal. It is increasingly demanded that the distribution of success and failure within one group be roughly comparable to that within other groups. It is not enough that all individuals start out on even terms, if the members of one group almost invariably end up well to the fore, and those of another far to the rear. This is what ethnic politics are all about in America, and in the main the Negro American demands are being put forth in this now traditional and established framework.[3]

Here a point of semantics must be grasped. The demand for Equality of Opportunity has been generally perceived by white Americans as a demand for liberty, a demand not to be excluded from the competitions of life—at the polling place, in the scholarship examinations, at the personnel office, on the housing market. Liberty does, of course, demand that everyone be free to try his luck, or test his skill in such matters. But these opportunities do not necessarily produce equality: on the contrary, to the extent that winners imply losers, equality of opportunity almost insures inequality of results.

The point of semantics is that equality of opportunity now has a different meaning for Negroes than it has for whites. It is not (or at least no longer) a demand for liberty alone, but also for equality—in terms of group results. In Bayard Rustin's terms, "It is now concerned not merely with removing the barriers to full *opportunity* but with achieving the fact of *equality*."[4] By equality Rustin means a distribution of achievements among Negroes roughly comparable to that among whites.

As Nathan Glazer has put it, "The demand for economic equality is now not the demand for equal opportunities for the equally qualified: it is now the demand for equality of economic results . . . The demand for equality in education...has also become a demand for equality of results, of outcomes."[5]

Some aspects of the new laws do guarantee results, in the sense that upon enactment and enforcement they bring about an objective that is an end in itself, e.g., the public accommodations title of the Civil Rights Act.

Other provisions are at once terminal and intermediary. The portions of the Civil Rights Act dealing with voting rights will achieve an objective that is an end in itself, but the exercise of those rights will no doubt lead to further enlargements of the freedom of the Negro American.

But by and large, the programs that have been enacted in the first phase of the Negro revolution—Manpower Retraining, the Job Corps, Community Action, et al.—only make opportunities available. They cannot insure the outcome.

The principal challenge of the next phase of the Negro revolution is to make certain that equality of results will now follow. If we do not, there will be no social peace in the United States for generations.

787-326 O-65—2

The Prospect for Equality

The time, therefore, is at hand for an unflinching look at the present potential of Negro Americans to move from where they now are to where they want, and ought to be.

There is no very satisfactory way, at present, to measure social health or social pathology within an ethnic, or religious, or geographical community. Data are few and uncertain, and conclusions drawn from them, including the conclusions that follow, are subject to the grossest error.* Nonetheless, the opportunities, no less than the dangers, of the present moment, demand that an assessment be made.

That being the case, it has to be said that there is a considerable body of evidence to support the conclusion that Negro social structure, in particular the Negro family, *battered and harassed by discrimination, injustice, and uprooting, is in the deepest trouble. While many young Negroes are moving ahead to unprecedented levels of achievement, many more are falling further and further behind.*

After an intensive study of the life of central Harlem, the board of directors of Harlem Youth Opportunities Unlimited, Inc. summed up their findings in one statement: "Massive deterioration of the fabric of society and its institutions..."[6]

It is the conclusion of this survey of the available national data, that what is true of central Harlem, can be said to be true of the Negro American world in general.

If this is so, it is the single most important social fact of the United States today.

---

*As much as possible, the statistics used in this paper refer to Negroes. However, certain data series are available only in terms of the white and nonwhite population. Where this is the case, the nonwhite data have been used as if they referred only to Negroes. This necessarily introduces some inaccuracies, but it does not appear to produce any significant distortions. In 1960, Negroes were 92.1 percent of all nonwhites. The remaining 7.9 percent is made up largely of Indians, Japanese, and Chinese. The combined male unemployment rates of these groups is lower than that of Negroes. In matters relating to family stability, the smaller groups are probably more stable. Thus 21 percent of Negro women who have ever married are separated, divorced, or their husbands are absent for other reasons. The comparable figure for Indians is 14 percent; Japanese, 7 percent; Chinese 6 percent. Therefore, the statistics on nonwhites generally *understate* the degree of disorganization of the Negro family and underemployment of Negro men.

Chapter II

The Negro American Family

At the heart of the deterioration of the fabric of Negro society is the deterioration of the Negro family.

It is the fundamental source of the weakness of the Negro community at the present time.

There is probably no single fact of Negro American life so little understood by whites. The Negro situation is commonly perceived by whites in terms of the visible manifestations of discrimination and poverty, in part because Negro protest is directed against such obstacles, and in part, no doubt, because these are facts which involve the actions and attitudes of the white community as well. It is more difficult, however, for whites to perceive the effect that three centuries of exploitation have had on the fabric of Negro society itself. Here the consequences of the historic injustices done to Negro Americans are silent and hidden from view. But here is where the true injury has occurred: unless this damage is repaired, all the effort to end discrimination and poverty and injustice will come to little.

The role of the family in shaping character and ability is so pervasive as to be easily overlooked. The family is the basic social unit of American life; it is the basic socializing unit. By and large, adult conduct in society is learned as a child.

A fundamental insight of psychoanalytic theory, for example, is that the child learns a way of looking at life in his early years through which all later experience is viewed and which profoundly shapes his adult conduct.

It may be hazarded that the reason family structure does not loom larger in public discussion of social issues is that people tend to assume that the nature of family life is about the same throughout American society. The mass media and the development of suburbia have created an image of the American family as a highly standardized phenomenon. It is therefore easy to assume that whatever it is that makes for differences among individuals or groups of individuals, it is not a different family structure.

There is much truth to this; as with any other nation, Americans are producing a recognizable family system. But that process is not completed by any means. There are still, for example, important differences in family patterns surviving from the age of the great European migration to the United States, and these variations account for notable differences in the progress and assimilation of various ethnic and religious groups.[7] A number of immigrant groups were characterized by unusually strong family bonds; these groups have characteristically progressed more rapidly than others.

But there is one truly great discontinuity in family structure in the United States at the present time: that between the white world in general and that of the Negro American.

The white family has achieved a high degree of stability and is maintaining that stability.

By contrast, the family structure of lower class Negroes is highly unstable, and in many urban centers is approaching complete breakdown.

N.b. There is considerable evidence that the Negro community is in fact dividing between a stable middle-class group that is steadily growing stronger and more successful, and an increasingly disorganized and disadvantaged lower-class group. There are indications, for example, that the middle-class Negro family puts a higher premium on family stability and the conserving of family resources than does the white middle-class family.[8] The discussion of this paper is not, obviously, directed to the first group excepting as it is affected by the experiences of the second—an important exception. (See Chapter IV, The Tangle of Pathology.)

There are two points to be noted in this context.

First, the emergence and increasing visibility of a Negro middle-class may beguile the nation into supposing that the circumstances of the remainder of the Negro community are equally prosperous, whereas just the opposite is true at present, and is likely to continue so.

Second, the lumping of all Negroes together in one statistical measurement very probably conceals the extent of the disorganization among the lower-class group. If conditions are improving for one and deteriorating for the other, the resultant statistical averages might show no change. Further, the statistics on the Negro family and most other subjects treated in this paper refer only to a specific point in time. They are a vertical measure of the situation at a given moment. They do not measure the experience of individuals over time. Thus the average monthly unemployment rate for Negro males for 1964 is recorded as 9 percent. But *during* 1964, some 29 percent of Negro males were unemployed at one time or another. Similarly, for example, if 36 percent of Negro children are living in broken homes *at any specific moment,* it is likely that a far higher proportion of Negro children find themselves in that situation *at one time or another* in their lives.

Nearly a Quarter of Urban Negro Marriages are Dissolved.

Nearly a quarter of Negro women living in cities who have ever married are divorced, separated, or are living apart from their husbands.

Percent Distribution of Ever-Married Females with Husbands Absent or Divorced, Rural-Urban, 1960

	Urban		Rural nonfarm		Rural farm	
	Nonwhite	white	Nonwhite	White	Nonwhite	White
Total, husbands absent or divorced	22.9	7.9	14.7	5.7	9.6	3.0
Total, husbands absent..	17.3	3.9	12.6	3.6	8.6	2.0
Separated............	12.7	1.8	7.8	1.2	5.6	0.5
Husbands absent for other reasons	4.6	2.1	4.8	2.4	3.0	1.5
Total, divorced.........	5.6	4.0	2.1	2.1	1.0	1.0

Source: *U.S. Census of Population, 1960, Nonwhite Population by Race,* PC (2) 1c, table 9, pp. 9-10.

The rates are highest in the urban North-east where 26 percent of Negro women ever married are either divorced, separated, or have their husbands absent.

On the urban frontier, the proportion of husbands absent is even higher. In New York City in 1960, it was 30.2 percent, *not* including divorces.

Among ever-married nonwhite women in the nation, the proportion with husbands present *declined* in *every* age group over the decade 1950-60, as follows:

Age	Percent with Husbands Present	
	1950	1960
15-19 years	77.8	72.5
20-24 years	76.7	74.2
25-29 years	76.1	73.4
30-34 years	74.9	72.0
35-39 years	73.1	70.7
40-44 years	68.9	68.2

Although similar declines occurred among white females, the proportion of white hus-bands present never dropped below 90 percent except for the first and last age group.[9]

Nearly One-Quarter of Negro Births are now Illegitimate.

Both white and Negro illegitimacy rates have been increasing, although from dramat-ically different bases. The white rate was 2 percent in 1940; it was 3.07 percent in 1963. In that period, the Negro rate went from 16.8 percent to 23.6 percent.

The number of illegitimate children per 1,000 live births increased by 11 among whites in the period 1940-63, but by 68 among non-whites. There are, of course, limits to the dependability of these statistics. There are almost certainly a considerable number of Negro children who, although technically ille-gitimate, are in fact the offspring of stable unions. On the other hand, it may be assumed that many births that are in fact illegitimate are recorded otherwise. Probably the two opposite effects cancel each other out.

Percent Distribution of Ever-Married Negro Females with Husbands Absent or Divorced, in Urban Areas, by Region, 1960

	Northeast	North Central	South	West
Total, husbands absent or divorced	25.6	22.6	21.5	24.7
Divorced.......................	3.9	7.3	4.8	9.9
Separated	16.0	11.7	11.9	10.7
Husbands absent for other reasons......................	5.7	3.6	4.8	4.1

Source: *U.S. Census of Population, 1960, Nonwhite Population by Race,* PC (2) 1c, table 9, pp. 9-10.

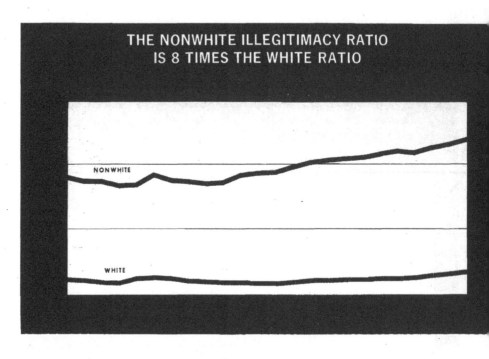

THE NONWHITE ILLEGITIMACY RATIO IS 8 TIMES THE WHITE RATIO

On the urban frontier, the nonwhite illegitimacy rates are usually higher than the national average, and the increase of late has been drastic.

In the District of Columbia, the illegitimacy rate for nonwhites grew from 21.8 percent in 1950, to 29.5 percent in 1964.

A similar picture of disintegrating Negro marriages emerges from the divorce statistics. Divorces have increased of late for both whites and nonwhites, but at a much greater rate for the latter. In 1940 both groups had a divorce rate of 2.2 percent. By 1964 the white rate had risen to 3.6 percent, but the nonwhite rate had reached 5.1 percent—40 percent greater than the formerly equal white rate.

Almost One-Fourth of Negro Families are Headed by Females.

As a direct result of this high rate of divorce, separation, and desertion, a very large percent of Negro families are headed by females. While the percentage of such families among whites has been dropping since 1940, it has been rising among Negroes.

The percent of nonwhite families headed by a female is more than double the percent for whites. Fatherless nonwhite families increased by a sixth between 1950 and 1960, but held constant for white families.

It has been estimated that only a minority of Negro children reach the age of 18 having lived all their lives with both their parents.

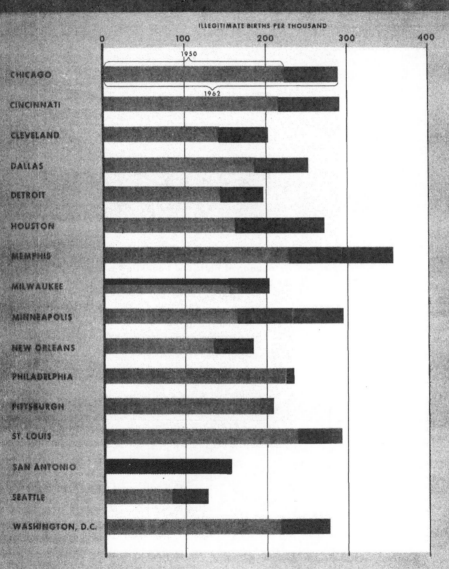

ILLEGITIMACY RATIOS PER 1,000 NONWHITE BIRTHS, BY CITY, 1950 AND 1962

ILLEGITIMATE BIRTHS PER THOUSAND

CHICAGO
CINCINNATI
CLEVELAND
DALLAS
DETROIT
HOUSTON
MEMPHIS
MILWAUKEE
MINNEAPOLIS
NEW ORLEANS
PHILADELPHIA
PITTSBURGH
ST. LOUIS
SAN ANTONIO
SEATTLE
WASHINGTON, D.C.

Source: See Appendix table 4.

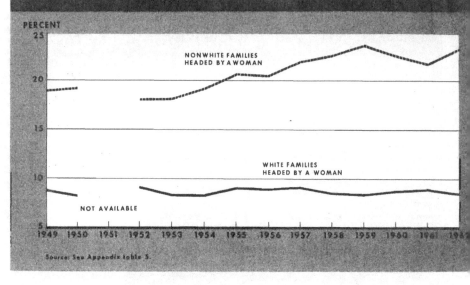

ALMOST ONE FOURTH OF NONWHITE FAMILIES
ARE HEADED BY A WOMAN

PERCENT

NONWHITE FAMILIES
HEADED BY A WOMAN

WHITE FAMILIES
HEADED BY A WOMAN

NOT AVAILABLE

1949 1950 1951 1952 1953 1954 1955 1956 1957 1958 1959 1960 1961 1962

Source: See Appendix table 5.

Percent Distribution of White and Nonwhite Families
in the United States, by Type of Family
1950 and 1960

Type of family	1960			1950		
	White	Non-white	Difference	White	Non-white	Difference
All families	100	100		100	100	
Husband-wife.......	88	74	14	87	78	9
Other male head....	3	5	−2	4	4	0
Female head.......	9	21	−12	9	18	−9

Source: *U.S. Census of Population, 1960, U.S. Summary (Detailed Characteristics)*,
table 186, p. 464.

787-326 O-65—3

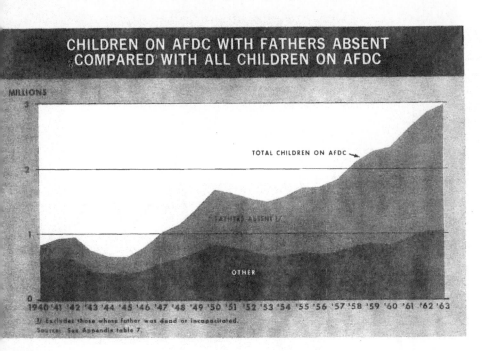

CHILDREN ON AFDC WITH FATHERS ABSENT COMPARED WITH ALL CHILDREN ON AFDC

MILLIONS

TOTAL CHILDREN ON AFDC →

FATHERS ABSENT 1/

OTHER

1940 '41 '42 '43 '44 '45 '46 '47 '48 '49 '50 '51 '52 '53 '54 '55 '56 '57 '58 '59 '60 '61 '62 '63

1/ Excludes those whose father was dead or incapacitated.
Source: See Appendix table 7.

Once again, this measure of family disorganization is found to be diminishing among white families and increasing among Negro families.

The Breakdown of the Negro Family Has Led to a Startling Increase in Welfare Dependency.

The majority of Negro children receive public assistance under the AFDC program at one point or another in their childhood.

At present, 14 percent of Negro children are receiving AFDC assistance, as against 2 percent of white children. Eight percent of white children receive such assistance at some time, as against 56 percent of non-whites, according to an extrapolation based on HEW data. (Let it be noted, however, that out of a total of 1.8 million nonwhite illegitimate children in the nation in 1961, 1.3 million were *not* receiving aid under the AFDC

program, although a substantial number have, or will, receive aid at some time in their lives.)

Again, the situation may be said to be worsening. The AFDC program, deriving from the long established Mothers' Aid programs, was established in 1935 principally to care for widows and orphans, although the legislation covered all children in homes deprived of parental support because one or both of their parents are absent or incapacitated.

In the beginning, the number of AFDC families in which the father was absent because of desertion was less than a third of the total. Today it is two-thirds. HEW estimates "that between two-thirds and three-fourths of the 50 percent increase from 1948 to 1955 in the number of absent-father families receiving ADC may be explained by an increase in broken homes in the population."[10]

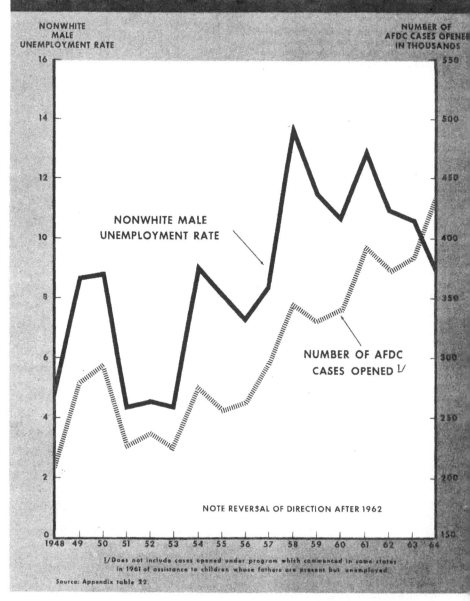

CASES OPENED UNDER AFDC COMPARED WITH UNEMPLOYMENT RATE FOR NONWHITE MALES

NONWHITE
MALE
UNEMPLOYMENT RATE

NUMBER OF
AFDC CASES OPENED
IN THOUSANDS

NONWHITE MALE
UNEMPLOYMENT RATE

NUMBER OF AFDC
CASES OPENED 1/

NOTE REVERSAL OF DIRECTION AFTER 1962

1/Does not include cases opened under program which commenced in some states
in 1961 of assistance to children whose fathers are present but unemployed.

Source: Appendix table 22.

- 13 -

A 1960 study of Aid to Dependent Children in Cook County, Ill.[11] stated:

> The 'typical' ADC mother in Cook County was married and had children by her husband, who deserted; his whereabouts are unknown, and he does not contribute to the support of his children. She is not free to remarry and has had an illegitimate child since her husband left. (Almost 90 percent of the ADC families are Negro.)[11]

The steady expansion of this welfare program, as of public assistance programs in general, can be taken as a measure of the steady disintegration of the Negro family structure over the past generation in the United States.

Chapter III

The Roots of the Problem

Slavery

The most perplexing question about American slavery, which has never been altogether explained, and which indeed most Americans hardly know exists, has been stated by Nathan Glazer as follows: "Why was American slavery the most awful the world has ever known?"[12] The only thing that can be said with certainty is that this is true: it was.

American slavery was profoundly different from, and in its lasting effects on individuals and their children, indescribably worse than, any recorded servitude, ancient or modern. The peculiar nature of American slavery was noted by Alexis de Tocqueville and others, but it was not until 1948 that Frank Tannenbaum, a South American specialist, pointed to the striking differences between Brazilian and American slavery. The feudal, Catholic society of Brazil had a legal and religious tradition which accorded the slave a place as a human being in the hierarchy of society—a luckless, miserable place, to be sure, but a place withal. In contrast, there was nothing in the tradition of English law or Protestant theology which could accommodate to the fact of human bondage—the slaves were therefore reduced to the status of chattels—often, no doubt, well cared for, even privileged chattels, but chattels nevertheless.

Glazer, also focusing on the Brazil-United States comparison, continues.

In Brazil, the slave had many more rights than in the United States: he could legally marry, he could, indeed had to, be baptized and become a member of the Catholic Church, his family could not be broken up for sale, and he had many days on which he could either rest or earn money to buy his freedom. The Government encouraged manumission, and the freedom of infants could often be purchased for a small sum at the baptismal font. In short: the Brazilian slave knew he was a man, and that he differed in degree, not in kind, from his master.[13]

[In the United States,] the slave was totally removed from the protection of organized society (compare the elaborate provisions for the protection of slaves in the Bible), his existence as a human being was given no recognition by any religious or secular agency, he was totally ignorant of and completely cut off from his past, and he was offered absolutely no hope for the future. His children could be sold, his marriage was not recognized, his wife could be violated or sold (there was something comic about calling the woman with whom the master permitted him to live a "wife"), and he could also be subject, without redress, to frightful barbarities—there were presumably as many sadists among slaveowners, men and women, as there are in other groups. The slave could not, by law, be taught to read or write; he could not practice any religion without the permission of his master, and could never meet with his fellows, for religious or any other purposes, except in the presence of a white; and finally, if a master wished to free him, every legal obstacle was used to thwart such action. This was not what slavery meant in the ancient world, in medieval and early modern Europe, or in Brazil and the West Indies.

More important, American slavery was also awful in its effects. If we compared the present situation of the American Negro with that of, let us say, Brazilian Negroes (who were slaves 20 years longer), we begin to suspect that the differences are the result of very different patterns of slavery. Today the Brazilian Negroes are Brazilians; though most are poor and do the hard and dirty work of the country, as Negroes do in the United States, they are not cut off from society. They reach into its highest strata, merging there—in smaller and smaller numbers, it is true, but with complete acceptance—with other Brazilians of all kinds. The relations between Negroes and whites in Brazil show nothing of the mass irrationality that prevails in this country.[14]

Stanley M. Elkins, drawing on the aberrant behavior of the prisoners in Nazi concentration camps, drew an elaborate parallel between the two institutions. This thesis has been summarized as follows by Thomas F. Pettigrew:

Both were closed systems, with little chance of manumission, emphasis on survival, and a single, omnipresent authority. The profound personality change created by Nazi internment, as independently reported by a number of psychologists and psychiatrists who survived, was toward childishness and total acceptance of the SS guards as father-figures—a syndrome strikingly similar to the "Sambo" caricature of the Southern slave. Nineteenth-century racists readily believed that the "Sambo" personality was simply an inborn racial type. Yet no African anthropological data have ever shown any personality type resembling Sambo; and the concentration camps molded the equivalent personality pattern in a wide variety of Caucasian prisoners. Nor was Sambo merely a product of "slavery" in the abstract, for the less devastating Latin American system never developed such a type.

Extending this line of reasoning, psychologists point out that slavery in all its forms sharply lowered the need for achievement in slaves...Negroes in bondage, stripped of their African heritage, were placed in a completely dependent role. All of their rewards came, not from individual initiative and enterprise, but from absolute obedience—a situation that severely depresses the need for achievement among all peoples. Most important of all, slavery vitiated family life... Since many slaveowners neither fostered Christian marriage among their slave couples nor hesitated to separate them on the auction block, the slave household often developed a fatherless matrifocal (mother-centered) pattern.[15]

The Reconstruction

With the emancipation of the slaves, the Negro American family began to form in the United States on a widespread scale. But it did so in an atmosphere markedly different from that which has produced the white American family.

The Negro was given liberty, but not equality. Life remained hazardous and marginal. Of the greatest importance, the Negro male, particularly in the South, became an object of intense hostility, an attitude unquestionably based in some measure on fear.

When Jim Crow made its appearance towards the end of the 19th century, it may be speculated that it was the Negro male who was most humiliated thereby; the male was more likely to use public facilities, which rapidly became segregated once the process began, and just as important, segregation, and the submissiveness it exacts, is surely more destructive to the male than to the female personality. Keeping the Negro "in his place" can be translated as keeping the Negro male in his place: the female was not a threat to anyone.

Unquestionably, these events worked against the emergence of a strong father figure. The very essence of the male animal, from the bantam rooster to the four-star general, is to strut. Indeed, in 19th century America, a particular type of exaggerated male boastfulness became almost a national style. Not for the Negro male. The "sassy nigger" was lynched.

In this situation, the Negro family made but little progress toward the middle-class pattern of the present time. Margaret Mead has pointed out that while "In every known human society, everywhere in the world, the young male learns that when he grows up one of the things which he must do in order to be a full member of society is to provide food for some female and her young."[16] This pattern is not immutable, however: it can be broken, even though it has always eventually reasserted itself.

> Within the family, each new generation of young males learn the appropriate nurturing behavior and superimpose upon their biologically given maleness this learned parental role. When the family breaks down—as it does under slavery, under certain forms of indentured labor and serfdom, in periods of extreme social unrest during wars, revolutions, famines, and epidemics, or in periods of abrupt transition from one type of economy to another—this delicate line of transmission is broken. Men may flounder badly in these periods, during which the primary unit may again become-mother and child, the biologically given, and the special conditions under which man has held his social traditions in trust are violated and distorted.[17]

E. Franklin Frazier makes clear that at the time of emancipation Negro women were already "accustomed to playing the dominant role in family and marriage relations" and that this role persisted in the decades of rural life that followed.

Urbanization

Country life and city life are profoundly different. The gradual shift of American society from a rural to an urban basis over the past century and a half has caused abundant strains, many of which are still much in evidence. When this shift occurs suddenly, drastically, in one or two generations, the effect is immensely disruptive of traditional social patterns.

It was this abrupt transition that produced the wild Irish slums of the 19th Century Northeast. Drunkenness, crime, corruption, discrimination, family disorganization, juvenile delinquency were the routine of that era. In our own time, the same sudden transition has produced the Negro slum—different from, but hardly better than its predecessors, and fundamentally the result of the same process.

Negroes are now more urbanized than whites.

Urban Population as Percent of Total, by Color, by Region, 1960

Region	White	Negro
United States	69.5	73.2
Northeast	79.1	95.7
North Central	66.8	95.7
South	58.6	58.4
West	77.6	92.6

Source: *U.S. Census of Population,* PC(1)-1D, 1960, *U.S. Summary,* table 155 and 233; PC (2)-1C, *Nonwhite Population by Race,* table 1.

Negro families in the cities are more frequently headed by a woman than those in the country. The difference between the white and Negro proportions of families headed by a woman is greater in the city than in the country.

Percent of Negro Families with Female Head, by Region and Area, 1960

Region	Urban	Rural Nonfarm	Rural Farm
United States	23.1	19.5	11.1
Northeast	24.2	14.1	4.3
North Central	20.8	14.7	8.4
South	24.2	20.0	11.2
West	20.7	9.4	5.5

Source: *U.S. Census of Population, 1960, Nonwhite Population by Race,* PC (2) 1C, table 9, pp. 9-10.

The promise of the city has so far been denied the majority of the Negro migrants, and most particularly the Negro family.

In 1939, E. Franklin Frazier described its plight movingly in that part of *The Negro Family* entitled "In the City of Destruction:"

The impact of hundreds of thousands of rural southern Negroes upon northern metropolitan communities presents a bewildering spectacle. Striking contrasts in levels of civilization and economic well-being among these newcomers to modern civilization seem to baffle any attempt to discover order and direction in their mode of life.[18]

In many cases, of course, the dissolution of the simple family organization has begun before the family reaches the northern city. But, if these families have managed to preserve their integrity until they reach the northern city, poverty, ignorance, and color force them to seek homes in deteriorated slum areas from which practically all institutional life has disappeared. Hence, at the same time that these simple rural families are losing their internal cohesion, they are being freed from the controlling force of public opinion and communal institutions. Family desertion among Negroes in cities appears, then, to be one of the inevitable consequences of the impact of urban life on the simple family organization and folk culture which the Negro has evolved in the rural South. The distribution of desertions in relation to the general economic and cultural organization of Negro communities that have grown up in our American cities shows in a striking manner the influence of selective factors in the process of adjustment to the urban environment.[19]

Frazier concluded his classic study, *The Negro Family*, with the prophesy that the "travail of civilization is not yet ended."

First, it appears that the family which evolved within the isolated world of the Negro folk will become increasingly disorganized. Modern means of communication will break down the isolation of the world of the black folk, and, as long as the bankrupt system of southern agriculture exists, Negro families will continue to seek a living in the towns and cities of the country. They will crowd the slum areas of southern cities or make their way to northern cities where their family life will become disrupted and their poverty will force them to depend upon charity.[20]

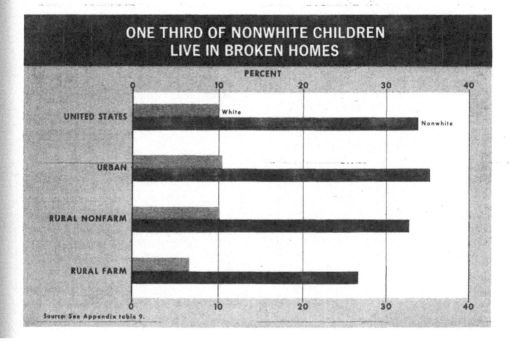

ONE THIRD OF NONWHITE CHILDREN LIVE IN BROKEN HOMES

PERCENT

UNITED STATES — White / Nonwhite

URBAN

RURAL NONFARM

RURAL FARM

Source: See Appendix table 9.

In every index of family pathology—divorce, separation, and desertion, female family head, children in broken homes, and illegitimacy— the contrast between the urban and rural environment for Negro families is unmistakable.

Harlem, into which Negroes began to move early in this century, is the center and symbol of the urban life of the Negro American. Conditions in Harlem are not worse, they are probably better than in most Negro ghettos. The social disorganization of central Harlem, comprising ten health areas, was thoroughly documented by the HARYOU report, save for the illegitimacy rates. These have now been made available to the Labor Department by the New York City Department of Health. There could hardly be a more dramatic demonstration of the crumbling—the breaking—of the family structure on the urban frontier.

Estimated Illegitimacy Ratios Per 1,000 Livebirths For Nonwhites In Central Harlem by Health Area, 1963

Health area [1]	Nonwhite
Total	434.1
No. 8	367.6
No. 10	488.9
No. 12	410.1
No. 13	422.5
No. 15	455.1
No. 16	449.4
No. 19	465.2
No. 24	424.8
No. 85.10	412.3
No. 85.20	430.8

[1] Statistics are reported by geographical areas designated "Health Areas."

Source: Department of Health, New York City.

Unemployment and Poverty

The impact of unemployment on the Negro family, and particularly on the Negro male, is the least understood of all the developments that have contributed to the present crisis. There is little analysis because there has been almost no inquiry. Unemployment, for whites and nonwhites alike, has on the whole been treated as an economic phenomenon, with almost no attention paid for at least a quarter-century to social and personal consequences.

In 1940, Edward Wight Bakke described the effects of unemployment on family structure in terms of six stages of adjustment.[21] Although the families studied were white, the pattern would clearly seem to be a general one, and apply to Negro families as well.

The first two stages end with the exhaustion of credit and the entry of the wife into the labor force. The father is no longer the provider and the elder children become resentful.

The third stage is the critical one of commencing a new day-to-day existence. At this point two women are in charge:

Consider the fact that relief investigators or case workers are normally women and deal with the housewife. Already suffering a loss in prestige and authority in the family because of his failure to be the chief bread winner, the male head of the family feels deeply this obvious transfer of planning for the family's well-being to two women, one of them an outsider. His role is reduced to that of errand boy to and from the relief office.[22]

If the family makes it through this stage Bakke finds that it is likely to survive, and the rest of the process is one of adjustment. *The critical element of adjustment was not welfare payments, but work.*

Having observed our families under conditions of unemployment with no public help, or with that help coming from direct [sic] and from work relief, we are convinced that after the exhaustion of self-produced resources, work relief is the only type of assistance which can restore the strained bonds of family relationship

- 19 -

in a way which promises the continued functioning of that family in meeting the responsibilities imposed upon it by our culture.[23]

Work is precisely the one thing the Negro family head in such circumstances has not received over the past generation.*

The fundamental, overwhelming fact is that *Negro unemployment*, with the exception of a few years during World War II and the Korean War, *has continued at disaster levels for 35 years.*

Once again, this is particularly the case in the northern urban areas to which the Negro population has been moving.

The 1930 Census (taken in the spring, before the depression was in full swing) showed Negro unemployment at 6.1 percent, as against 6.6 percent for whites. But taking out the South reversed the relationship: white 7.4 percent, nonwhite 11.5 percent.

By 1940, the 2 to 1 white-Negro unemployment relationship that persists to this day had clearly emerged. Taking out the South again, whites were 14.8 percent, nonwhites 29.7 percent.

*An exception is the rather small impact of the ADC-U program since 1961, now expanded by Title V of the Economic Opportunity Act.

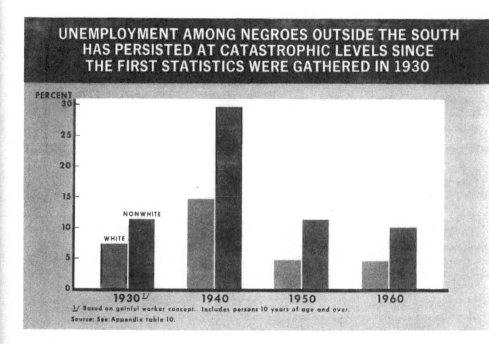

UNEMPLOYMENT AMONG NEGROES OUTSIDE THE SOUTH HAS PERSISTED AT CATASTROPHIC LEVELS SINCE THE FIRST STATISTICS WERE GATHERED IN 1930

PERCENT

NONWHITE

WHITE

1930 1/   1940   1950   1960

1/ Based on gainful worker concept. Includes persons 10 years of age and over.
Source: See Appendix table 10.

Since 1929, the Negro worker has been tremendously affected by the movements of the business cycle and of employment. He has been hit worse by declines than whites, and proportionately helped more by recoveries.

From 1951 to 1963, the level of Negro male unemployment was on a long-run rising trend, while at the same time following the short-run ups and downs of the business cycle. During the same period, the number of broken families in the Negro world was also on a long-run rise, with intermediate ups and downs.

A glance at the chart on page 22 reveals that the series move in the same directions—up and down together, with a long-run rising trend—but that the peaks and troughs are 1 year out of phase. Thus unemployment peaks 1 year before broken families, and so on. By plotting these series in terms of deviation from trend, and moving the unemployment curve *1 year ahead,* we see the clear relation of the two otherwise seemingly unrelated series of events; the cyclical swings in unemployment have their counterpart in increases and decreases in separations.

The effect of recession unemployment on divorces further illustrates the economic roots of the problem. The nonwhite divorce rates dipped slightly in high unemployment years like 1954-55, 1958, and 1961-62. (See table 21 on page 77 .)

Divorce is expensive: those without money resort to separation or desertion. While divorce is not a desirable goal for a society, it recognizes the importance of marriage and family, and for children some family continuity and support is more likely when the institution of the family has been so recognized.

The conclusion from these and similar data is difficult to avoid: During times when jobs were reasonably plentiful (although at no time during this period, save perhaps the first 2 years, did the unemployment rate for

Negro males drop to anything like a reasonable level) the Negro family became stronger and more stable. As jobs became more and more difficult to find, the stability of the family became more and more difficult to maintain.

This relation is clearly seen in terms of the illegitimacy rates of census tracts in the District of Columbia compared with male unemployment rates in the same neighborhoods.

In 1963, a prosperous year, 29.2 percent of all Negro men in the labor force were unemployed at some time during the year. Almost half of these men were out of work 15 weeks or more.

The impact of poverty on Negro family structure is no less obvious, although again it may not be widely acknowledged. There would seem to be an American tradition, agrarian in its origins but reinforced by attitudes of urban immigrant groups, to the effect that family morality and stability decline as income and social position rise. Over the years this may have provided some consolation to the poor, but there is little evidence that it is true. On the contrary, higher family incomes are unmistakably associated with greater family stability—which comes first may be a matter for conjecture, but the conjunction of the two characteristics is unmistakable.

The Negro family is no exception. In the District of Columbia, for example, census tracts with median incomes over $8,000 had an illegitimacy rate one-third that of tracts in the category under $4,000.

The Wage System

The American wage system is conspicuous in the degree to which it provides high incomes for individuals, but is rarely adjusted to insure that family, as well as individual needs are met. Almost without exception, the social welfare and social insurance systems of other industrial democracies provide for some adjustment or supplement of a

UNEMPLOYMENT RATE OF NONWHITE MEN COMPARED WITH PERCENT OF NONWHITE WOMEN SEPARATED FROM HUSBANDS

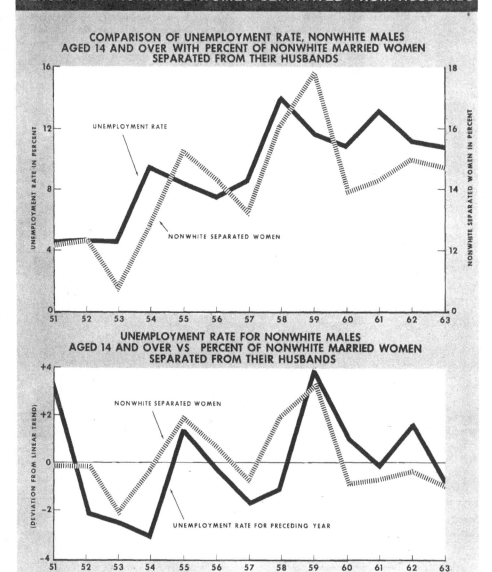

COMPARISON OF UNEMPLOYMENT RATE, NONWHITE MALES
AGED 14 AND OVER WITH PERCENT OF NONWHITE MARRIED WOMEN
SEPARATED FROM THEIR HUSBANDS

UNEMPLOYMENT RATE

NONWHITE SEPARATED WOMEN

UNEMPLOYMENT RATE FOR NONWHITE MALES
AGED 14 AND OVER VS PERCENT OF NONWHITE MARRIED WOMEN
SEPARATED FROM THEIR HUSBANDS

NONWHITE SEPARATED WOMEN

UNEMPLOYMENT RATE FOR PRECEDING YEAR

Source: See Appendix table 11 and 12.

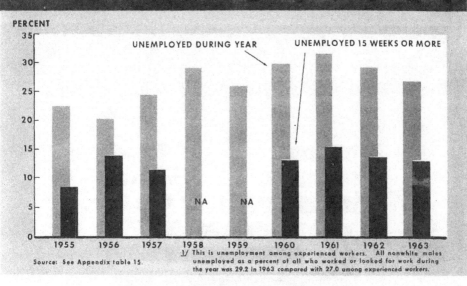

AMONG NONWHITE MEN WORKING DURING THE YEAR, ONE-FOURTH OR MORE EXPERIENCE UNEMPLOYMENT [1]

PERCENT

UNEMPLOYED DURING YEAR   UNEMPLOYED 15 WEEKS OR MORE

1955 1956 1957 1958 1959 1960 1961 1962 1963

NA   NA

Source: See Appendix table 15.

[1] This is unemployment among experienced workers. All nonwhite males unemployed as a percent of all who worked or looked for work during the year was 29.2 in 1963 compared with 27.0 among experienced workers.

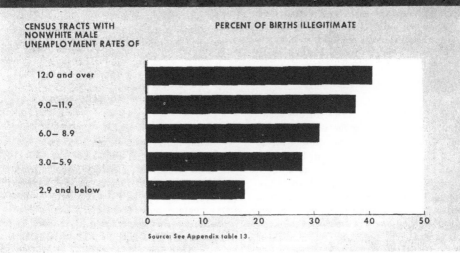

PERCENT OF NONWHITE ILLEGITIMATE BIRTHS IN 1963 IN DISTRICT OF COLUMBIA CENSUS TRACTS AS RELATED TO NONWHITE 1960 UNEMPLOYMENT RATE OF CENSUS TRACT

CENSUS TRACTS WITH NONWHITE MALE UNEMPLOYMENT RATES OF

PERCENT OF BIRTHS ILLEGITIMATE

12.0 and over

9.0—11.9

6.0— 8.9

3.0—5.9

2.9 and below

0   10   20   30   40   50

Source: See Appendix table 13.

- 23 -

PERCENT OF NONWHITE ILLEGITIMATE BIRTHS IN 1963 IN D.C. CENSUS TRACTS AS RELATED TO MEDIAN NONWHITE FAMILY INCOME IN 1959 OF CENSUS TRACT [1/]

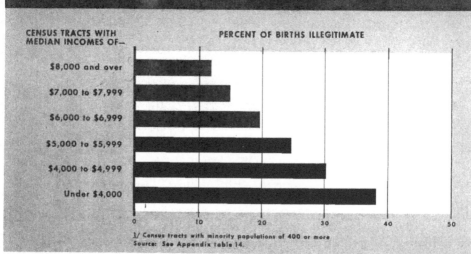

CENSUS TRACTS WITH MEDIAN INCOMES OF—

PERCENT OF BIRTHS ILLEGITIMATE

- $8,000 and over
- $7,000 to $7,999
- $6,000 to $6,999
- $5,000 to $5,999
- $4,000 to $4,999
- Under $4,000

0   10   20   30   40   50

[1/] Census tracts with minority populations of 400 or more.
Source: See Appendix table 14.

worker's income to provide for the extra expenses of those with families. American arrangements do not, save for income tax deductions.

The Federal minimum wage of $1.25 per hour provides a basic income for an individual, but an income well below the poverty line for a couple, much less a family with children.

The 1965 Economic Report of the President revised the data on the number of persons living in poverty in the United States to take account of the varying needs of families of different sizes, rather than using a flat cut off at the $3,000 income level. The resulting revision illustrates the significance of family size. Using these criteria, the number of poor families is smaller, but the number of large families who are poor increases, and the number of children in poverty rises by more than one-third—from 11 million to 15 million. This means that one-fourth of the Nation's children live in families that are poor. [24]

A third of these children belong to families in which the father was not only present, but was employed the year round. In overall terms, median family income is lower for large families than for small families. Families of six or more children have median incomes 24 percent below families with three. (It may be added that 47 percent of young men who fail the Selective Service education test come from families of six or more.)

During the 1950-60 decade of heavy Negro migration to the cities of the North and West, the ratio of nonwhite to white family income in cities increased from 57 to 63 percent. Corresponding declines in the ratio in the rural nonfarm and farm areas kept the national ratio virtually unchanged. But between 1960 and 1963, median nonwhite family income slipped from 55 percent to 53 percent of white income. The drop occurred in three regions, with only the South, where a larger proportion of Negro families have more than one earner, showing a slight improvement.

Ratio of Nonwhite to White Family Median Income, United States and Regions, 1960-63

Region	1960	1961	1962	1963
United States..	55	53	53	53
Northeast ...	68	67	66	65
North Central.	74	72	68	73
South	43	43	47	45
West	81	87	73	76

Source: U. S. Department of Commerce. Bureau of the Census, Current Population Reports, Series P-60, *Income of Families and Persons in the United States*, No. 37 (1960), No. 39 (1961), No. 41 (1962), No. 43 (1963). Data by region, table 11 in P-60, No. 41, for 1962, table 13 in P-60, No. 43, for 1963 and, for 1960 and 1961, unpublished tabulations from the Current Population Survey.

Because in general terms Negro families have the largest number of children and the lowest incomes, many Negro fathers literally cannot support their families. Because the father is either not present, is unemployed, or makes such a low wage, the Negro woman goes to work. Fifty-six percent of Negro women, age 25 to 64, are in the work force, against 42 percent of white women. This dependence on the mother's income undermines the position of the father and deprives the children of the kind of attention, particularly in school matters, which is now a standard feature of middle-class upbringing.

The Dimensions Grow

The dimensions of the problems of Negro Americans are compounded by the present extraordinary growth in Negro population. At the founding of the nation, and into the first decade of the 19th century, 1 American in 5 was a Negro. The proportion declined steadily until it was only 1 in 10 by 1920, where it held until the 1950's, when it began to rise. Since 1950, the Negro population

has grown at a rate of 2.4 percent per year compared with 1.7 percent for the total population. If this rate continues, in seven years 1 American in 8 will be nonwhite.

These changes are the result of a declining Negro death rate, now approaching that of the nation generally, and a fertility rate that grew steadily during the postwar period. By 1959, the ratio of white to nonwhite fertility rates reached 1:1.42. Both the white and nonwhite fertility rates have declined since 1959, but the differential has not narrowed.

Family size increased among nonwhite families between 1950 and 1960—as much for those without fathers as for those with fathers. Average family size changed little among white families, with a slight increase in the size of husband-wife families balanced by a decline in the size of families without fathers.

Average Number of Family Members by Type of Family and Color, Conterminous United States, 1960 and 1950

Type of family	1950		1960	
	White	Non-white	White	Non-white
All families...	3.54	4.07	3.58	4.30
Husband-wife..	3.61	4.16	3.66	4.41
Other male head	3.05	3.63	2.82	3.56
Female head ..	3.06	3.82	2.93	4.04

Source: *U.S. Census of Population, 1960, U.S. Summary (Detailed Characteristics)*, table 187, p. 469.

Negro women not only have more children, but have them earlier. Thus in 1960, there were 1,247 children ever born per thousand ever-married nonwhite women 15 to 19 years of age, as against only 725 among white women, a ratio of 1.7:1. The Negro fertility rate overall is now 1.4 times the white, but what might be called the generation rate is 1.7 times the white.

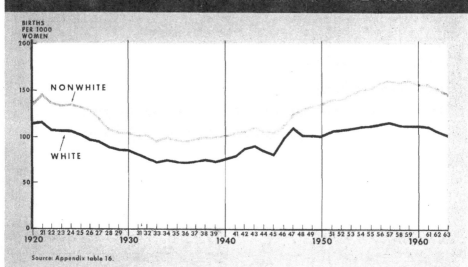

FERTILITY RATES FOR NONWHITE WOMEN ARE ONE-THIRD HIGHER THAN THOSE FOR WHITE WOMEN

BIRTHS
PER 1000
WOMEN

NONWHITE

WHITE

Source: Appendix table 16.

This population growth must inevitably lead to an unconcealable crisis in Negro unemployment. The most conspicuous failure of the American social system in the past 10 years has been its inadequacy in providing jobs for Negro youth. Thus, in January 1965 the unemployment rate for Negro teenagers stood at 29 percent. This problem will now become steadily more serious.

Population and Labor Force Projections, by Color

	Percent increase	
	Actual 1954-64	Projected* 1964-70
Civilian population age 14 and over		
White	15.6	9.7
Nonwhite	23.9	19.9
Civilian labor force		
White	14.6	10.8
*Nonwhite	19.3	20.0

*Population and labor force projections by color were made by the Bureau of Labor Statistics. They have not been revised since the total population and labor force were re-estimated, but are considered accurate measures of the relative magnitudes of increase.

Source: Bureau of Labor Statistics.

During the rest of the 1960's the nonwhite civilian population 14 years of age and over will increase by 20 percent—more than double the white rate. The nonwhite labor force will correspondingly increase 20 percent in the next 6 years, double the rate of increase in the nonwhite labor force of the past decade.

Family income in 1959	Number of Children per Nonwhite Mother Age 35-39, 1960
Under $2,000	5.3
$2,000 to $3,999	4.3
$4,000 to $4,999	4.0
$5,000 to $5,999	3.8
$6,000 to $6,999	3.5
$7,000 to $9,999	3.2
$10,000 to $14,999	2.9
$15,000 and over	2.9

Source: 1960 Census, *Women by Number of Children Ever Born,* PC (2) 3A, table 38, p. 188.

As with the population as a whole, there is much evidence that children are being born most rapidly in those Negro families with the least financial resources. This is an ancient pattern, but because the needs of children are greater today it is very possible that the education and opportunity gap between the offspring of these families and those of stable middle-class unions is not closing, but is growing wider.

A cycle is at work; too many children too early make it most difficult for the parents to finish school. (In February, 1963, 38 percent of the white girls who dropped out of school did so because of marriage or pregnancy, as against 49 percent of nonwhite girls.)[25] An Urban League study in New York reported that 44 percent of girl dropouts left school because of pregnancy.[26]

Low education levels in turn produce low income levels, which deprive children of many opportunities, and so the cycle repeats itself.

Chapter IV

The Tangle of Pathology

That the Negro American has survived at all is extraordinary—a lesser people might simply have died out, as indeed others have. That the Negro community has not only survived, but in this political generation has entered national affairs as a moderate, humane, and constructive national force is the highest testament to the healing powers of the democratic ideal and the creative vitality of the Negro people.

But it may not be supposed that the Negro American community has not paid a fearful price for the incredible mistreatment to which it has been subjected over the past three centuries.

In essence, the Negro community has been forced into a matriarchal structure which, because it is so out of line with the rest of the American society, seriously retards the progress of the group as a whole, and imposes a crushing burden on the Negro male and, in consequence, on a great many Negro women as well.

There is, presumably, no special reason why a society in which males are dominant in family relationships is to be preferred to a matriarchal arrangement. However, it is clearly a disadvantage for a minority group to be operating on one principle, while the great majority of the population, and the one with the most advantages to begin with, is operating on another. This is the present situation of the Negro. Ours is a society which presumes male leadership in private and public affairs. The arrangements of society facilitate such leadership and reward it. A subculture, such as that of the Negro American, in which this is not the pattern, is placed at a distinct disadvantage.

Here an earlier word of caution should be repeated. There is much evidence that a considerable number of Negro families have managed to break out of the tangle of pathology and to establish themselves as stable, effective units, living according to patterns of American society in general. E. Franklin Frazier has suggested that the middle-class Negro American family is, if anything, more patriarchal and protective of its children than the general run of such families.[27] Given equal opportunities, the children of these families will perform as well or better than their white peers. They need no help from anyone, and ask none.

While this phenomenon is not easily measured, one index is that middle-class Negroes have even fewer children than middle-class whites, indicating a desire to conserve the advances they have made and to insure that their children do as well or better. Negro women who marry early to uneducated laborers have more children than white women in the same situation; Negro women who marry at the common age for the middle class to educated men doing technical or professional work have only four-fifths as many children as their white counterparts.

It might be estimated that as much as half of the Negro community falls into the middle class. However, the remaining half is in desperate and deteriorating circumstances. Moreover, because of housing segregation it is immensely difficult for the stable half to escape from the cultural influences of the unstable one. The children of middle-class Negroes often as not must grow up in, or next to the slums, an experience almost unknown to white middle-class children. They are therefore constantly exposed to the pathology of the disturbed group and constantly

Children Born per Woman Age 35 to 44: Wives of Uneducated Laborers
who Married Young, Compared with Wives of Educated Professional
Workers who Married After Age 21, White and Nonwhite, 1960[1]

	Children per Woman	
	White	Nonwhite
Wives married at age 14 to 21 to husbands who are laborers and did not go to high school	3.8	4.7
Wives married at age 22 or over to husbands who are professional or technical workers and have completed 1 year or more of college	2.4	1.9

[1]Wives married only once, with husbands present.

Source: 1960 Census, *Women by Number of Children ever Born*, PC (2) 3A, table 39 and 40,
pp. 199-238.

in danger of being drawn into it. It is for this reason that the propositions put forth in this study may be thought of as having a more or less general application.

In a word, most Negro youth are in *danger* of being caught up in the tangle of pathology that affects their world, and probably a majority are so entrapped. Many of those who escape do so for one generation only: as things now are, their children may have to run the gauntlet all over again. That is not the least vicious aspect of the world that white America has made for the Negro.

Obviously, not every instance of social pathology afflicting the Negro community can be traced to the weakness of family structure. If, for example, organized crime in the Negro community were not largely controlled by whites, there would be more capital accumulation among Negroes, and therefore probably more Negro business enterprises. If it were not for the hostility and fear many whites exhibit towards Negroes, they in turn would be less afflicted by hostility and fear and so on. There is no one Negro community. There is no one Negro problem. There is no one solution. Nonetheless, at the center of the tangle of pathology is the weakness of the family structure. Once or twice removed, it will be found to be the principal source of most of the aberrant, inadequate, or anti-social behavior that did not establish, but now serves to perpetuate the cycle of poverty and deprivation.

It was by destroying the Negro family under slavery that white America broke the will of the Negro people. Although that will has re-asserted itself in our time, it is a resurgence doomed to frustration unless the viability of the Negro family is restored.

Matriarchy

A fundamental fact of Negro American family life is the often reversed roles of husband and wife.

Robert O. Blood, Jr. and Donald M. Wolfe, in a study of Detroit families, note that "Negro husbands have unusually low power,"[28] and while this is characteristic of all low income families, the pattern pervades the Negro social structure: "the cumulative result of discrimination in jobs..., the segregated housing, and the poor schooling of Negro men."[29] In 44 percent of the Negro families studied, the wife was dominant, as against 20 percent of white wives. "Whereas the majority of white families are equalitarian, the largest percentage of Negro families are dominated by the wife."[30]

The matriarchal pattern of so many Negro families reinforces itself over the generations. This process begins with education. Although the gap appears to be closing at the moment, for a long while, Negro females were better educated than Negro males, and this remains true today for the Negro population as a whole.

Educational Attainment of the Civilian Noninstitutional Population 18 Years of Age and Over, March 1964

Color and sex	Median school years completed
White:	
Male	12.1
Female . . .	12.1
Nonwhite:	
Male	9.2
Female . . .	10.0

Source: Bureau of Labor Statistics, unpublished data.

The difference in educational attainment between nonwhite men and women in the labor force is even greater; men lag 1.1 years behind women.

The disparity in educational attainment of male and female youth age 16 to 21 who were out of school in February 1963, is striking. Among the nonwhite males, 66.3 percent were not high school graduates, compared with 55.0 percent of the females. A similar difference existed at the college level, with 4.5 percent of the males having completed 1 to 3 years of college compared with 7.3 percent of the females.

The poorer performance of the male in school exists from the very beginning, and the magnitude of the difference was documented by the 1960 Census in statistics on the number of children who have fallen one

or more grades below the typical grade for children of the same age. The boys have more frequently fallen behind at every age level. (White boys also lag behind white girls, but at a differential of 1 to 6 percentage points.)

Percent of Nonwhite Youth Enrolled in School Who are 1 or More Grades Below Mode for Age, by Sex, 1960

Age	Male	Female
7 to 9 years old	7.8	5.8
10 to 13 years old	25.0	17.1
14 and 15 years old	35.5	24.8
16 and 17 years old	39.4	27.2
18 and 19 years old	57.3	46.0

Source: 1960 Census, *School Enrollment*, PC(2) 5A, table 3, p. 24.

In 1960, 39 percent of all white persons 25 years of age and over who had completed 4 or more years of college were women. Fifty-three percent of the nonwhites who had attained this level were women.

However, the gap is closing. By October 1963, there were slightly more Negro men in college than women. Among whites there were almost twice as many men as women enrolled.

There is much evidence that Negro females are better students than their male counterparts.

Daniel Thompson of Dillard University, in a private communication on January 9, 1965, writes:

As low as is the aspirational level among lower class Negro girls, it is considerably higher than among the boys. For example, I have examined the honor rolls in Negro high schools for about 10 years. As a rule, from 75 to 90 percent of all Negro honor students are girls.

Fall Enrollment of Civilian Noninstitutional Population in College,
by Color and Sex - October 1963
(in thousands)

Color and Sex	Population, age 14-34, Oct. 1, 1963	Number enrolled	Percent of youth, age 14-34
Nonwhite			
Male	2,884	149	5.2
Female.	3,372	137	4.1
White			
Male	21,700	2,599	12.0
Female	20,613	1,451	7.0

Source: U.S. Bureau of the Census, *Current Population Reports,* Series P-20, No. 129 July 24, 1964, tables 1, 5.

Dr. Thompson reports that 70 percent of all applications for the National Achievement Scholarship Program financed by the Ford Foundation for outstanding Negro high school graduates are girls, despite special efforts by high school principals to submit the names of boys.

The finalists for this new program for outstanding Negro students were recently announced. Based on an inspection of the names, only about 43 percent of all the 639 finalists were male. (However, in the regular National Merit Scholarship program, males received 67 percent of the 1964 scholarship awards.)

Inevitably, these disparities have carried over to the area of employment and income.

In 1 out of 4 Negro families where the husband is present, is an earner, and someone else in the family works, the husband is not the principal earner. The comparable figure for whites is 18 percent.

More important, it is clear that Negro females have established a strong position for themselves in white collar and professional employment, precisely the areas of the economy which are growing most rapidly, and to which the highest prestige is accorded.

The President's Committee on Equal Employment Opportunity, making a preliminary report on employment in 1964 of over 16,000 companies with nearly 5 million employees, revealed this pattern with dramatic emphasis.

In this work force, Negro males outnumber Negro females by a ratio of 4 to 1. Yet Negro males represent only 1.2 percent of all males in white collar occupations, while Negro females represent 3.1 percent of the total female white collar work force. Negro males represent 1.1 percent of all male professionals, whereas Negro females represent roughly 6 percent of all female professionals. Again, in technician occupations, Negro males represent 2.1 percent of all male technicians while Negro females represent roughly 10 percent of all female technicians. It would appear therefore that there are proportionately 4 times as many Negro females in significant white collar jobs than Negro males.

Although it is evident that office and clerical jobs account for approximately 50 percent of all Negro female white collar

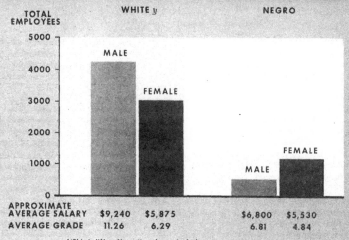

**DEPARTMENT OF LABOR EMPLOYMENT
AS OF DECEMBER 31, 1964**

	WHITE 1/			NEGRO	
TOTAL EMPLOYEES	MALE / FEMALE			MALE / FEMALE	
APPROXIMATE AVERAGE SALARY	$9,240	$5,875		$6,800	$5,530
AVERAGE GRADE	11.26	6.29		6.81	4.84

1/This is "Non-Negro" and may include some nonwhites other than Negro.
Source: See Appendix table 17.

workers, it is significant that 6 out of every 100 Negro females are in professional jobs. This is substantially similar to the rate of all females in such jobs. Approximately 7 out of every 100 Negro females are in technician jobs. This exceeds the proportion of all females in technician jobs—approximately 5 out of every 100.

Negro females in skilled jobs are almost the same as that of all females in such jobs. Nine out of every 100 Negro males are in skilled occupations while 21 out of 100 of all males are in such jobs.[31]

This pattern is to be seen in the Federal government, where special efforts have been made recently to insure equal employment opportunity for Negroes. These efforts have been notably successful in Departments such as Labor, where some 19 percent of employees are now Negro. (A not disproportionate per-

centage, given the composition of the work force in the areas where the main Department offices are located.) However, it may well be that these efforts have redounded mostly to the benefit of Negro women, and may even have accentuated the comparative disadvantage of Negro men. Seventy percent of the Negro employees of the Department of Labor are women, as contrasted with only 42 percent of the white employees.

Among nonprofessional Labor Department employees—where the most employment opportunities exist for all groups—Negro women outnumber Negro men 4 to 1, and average almost one grade higher in classification.

The testimony to the effects of these patterns in Negro family structure is widespread, and hardly to be doubted.

Whitney Young:

Historically, in the matriarchal Negro society, mothers made sure that if one of their children had a chance for higher education the daughter was the one to pursue it. [32]

The effect on family functioning and role performance of this historical experience [economic deprivation] is what you might predict. Both as a husband and as a father the Negro male is made to feel inadequate, not because he is unlovable or unaffectionate, lacks intelligence or even a gray flannel suit. But in a society that measures a man by the size of his pay check, he doesn't stand very tall in a comparison with his white counterpart. To this situation he may react with withdrawal, bitterness toward society, aggression both within the family and racial group, self-hatred, or crime. Or he may escape through a number of avenues that help him to lose himself in fantasy or to compensate for his low status through a variety of exploits. [33]

Thomas Pettigrew:

The Negro wife in this situation can easily become disgusted with her financially dependent husband, and her rejection of him further alienates the male from family life. Embittered by their experiences with men, many Negro mothers often act to perpetuate the mother-centered pattern by taking a greater interest in their daughters than their sons. [34]

Deton Brooks:

In a matriarchal structure, the women are transmitting the culture. [35]

Dorothy Height:

If the Negro woman has a major underlying concern, it is the status of the Negro man and his position in the community and his need for feeling himself an important person, free and able to make his contribution in the whole society in order that he may strengthen his home. [36]

Duncan M. MacIntyre:

The Negro illegitimacy rate always has been high—about eight times the white rate in 1940 and somewhat higher today even though the white illegitimacy rate also is climbing. The Negro statistics are symtomatic of some old socioeconomic problems, not the least of which are underemployment among Negro men and compensating higher labor force propensity among Negro women. Both operate to enlarge the mother's role, undercutting the status of the male and making many Negro families essentially matriarchal. The Negro man's uncertain employment prospects, matriarchy, and the high cost of divorces combine to encourage desertion (the poor man's divorce), increases the number of couples not married, and thereby also increases the Negro illegitimacy rate. In the meantime, higher Negro birth rates are increasing the nonwhite population, while migration into cities like Detroit, New York, Philadelphia, and Washington, D.C. is making the public assistance rolls in such cities heavily, even predominantly, Negro. [37]

Robin M. Williams, Jr. in a study of Elmira, New York:

Only 57 percent of Negro adults reported themselves as married—spouse present, as compared with 78 percent of native white American gentiles, 91 percent of Italian-American, and 96 percent of Jewish informants. Of the 93 unmarried Negro youths interviewed, 22 percent did not have their mother living in the home with them, and 42 percent reported that their father was not living in their home. One-third of the youths did not know their father's present occupation, and two-thirds of a sample of 150 Negro adults did not know what the occupation of their father's father had been. Forty percent of the youths said that they had brothers and sisters living in other communities; another 40 percent reported relatives living in their home who were not parents, siblings, or grandparent. [38]

The Failure of Youth

Williams' account of Negro youth growing up with little knowledge of their fathers, less of their fathers' occupations, still less of family occupational traditions, is in sharp contrast to the experience of the white child.

The white family, despite many variants, remains a powerful agency not only for transmitting property from one generation to the next, but also for transmitting no less valuable contracts with the world of education and work. In an earlier age, the Carpenters, Wainwrights, Weavers, Mercers, Farmers, Smiths acquired their names as well as their trades from their fathers and grandfathers. Children today still learn the patterns of work from their fathers even though they may no longer go into the same jobs.

White children without fathers at least perceive all about them the pattern of men working.

Negro children without fathers flounder—and fail.

Not always, to be sure. The Negro community produces its share, very possibly more than its share, of young people who have the something extra that carries them over the worst obstacles. But such persons are always a minority. The common run of young people in a group facing serious obstacles to success do not succeed.

A prime index of the disadvantage of Negro youth in the United States is their consistently poor performance on the mental tests that are a standard means of measuring ability and performance in the present generation.

There is absolutely no question of any genetic differential: Intelligence potential is distributed among Negro infants in the same proportion and pattern as among Icelanders or Chinese or any other group. American society, however, impairs the Negro potential. The statement of the HARYOU report that "there is no basic disagreement over the fact that central Harlem students are performing poorly in school"[39] may be taken as true of Negro slum children throughout the United States.

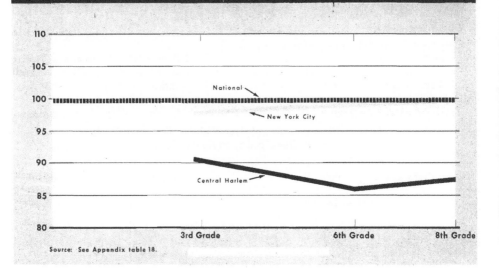

BY THE 8th GRADE, CENTRAL HARLEM PUPILS' AVERAGE IQ WAS 87.7 COMPARED TO THE NATIONAL NORM OF 100

Source: See Appendix table 18.

Eighth grade children in central Harlem have a median IQ of 87.7, which means that perhaps a third of the children are scoring at levels perilously near to those of retardation. IQ *declines* in the first decade of life, rising only slightly thereafter.

The effect of broken families on the performance of Negro youth has not been extensively measured, but studies that have been made show an unmistakable influence.

Martin Deutch and Bert Brown, investigating intelligence test differences between Negro and white 1st and 5th graders of different social classes, found that there is a direct relationship between social class and IQ. As the one rises so does the other: but more for whites than Negroes. This is surely a result of housing segregation, referred to earlier, which makes it difficult for middle-class Negro families to escape the slums.

The authors explain that "it is much more difficult for the Negro to attain identical middle- or upper-middle-class status with whites, and the social class gradations are less marked for Negroes because Negro life in a caste society is considerably more homogeneous than is life for the majority group."[40]

Therefore, the authors look for background variables other than social class which might explain the difference: "One of the most striking differences between the Negro and white groups is the consistently higher frequency of broken homes and resulting family disorganization in the Negro group."[41]

Father Absent From the Home

Lowest social class level		Middle social class level		Highest social class level	
Percent of		Percent of		Percent of	
White	Negro	White	Negro	White	Negro
15.4	43.9	10.3	27.9	0.0	13.7

(Adapted from authors' table)

Further, they found that children from homes where fathers are present have significantly higher scores than children in homes without fathers.

	Mean Intelligence Scores
Father Present	97.83
Father Absent	90.79

The influence of the father's presence was then tested *within* the social classes and school grades for Negroes alone. They found that "a consistent trend within both

Mean Intelligence Scores of Negro Children by School, Grade, Social Class, and by Presence of Father

Social Class and School Grade	Father present	Father absent
Lowest social class level:		
Grade 1	95.2	87.8
Grade 5	92.7	85.7
Middle social class level:		
Grade 1	98.7	92.8
Grade 5	92.9	92.0

(Adapted from authors' table)

Percent of Nonwhite Males Enrolled in School, by Age and Presence of Parents, 1960

Age	Both parents present	One parent present	Neither parent present
5 years	41.7	44.2	34.3
6 years	79.3	78.7	73.8
7 to 9 years	96.1	95.3	93.9
10 to 13 years	96.2	95.5	93.0
14 and 15 years	91.8	89.9	85.0
16 and 17 years.	78.0	72.7	63.2
18 and 19 years.	46.5	40.0	32.3

Source: 1960 Census, *School Enrollment*, PC (2) 5A, table 3, p. 24.

grades at the lower SES [social class] level appears, and in no case is there a reversal of this trend: for males, females, and the combined group, the IQ's of children with fathers in the home are always higher than those who have no father in the home." [42]

The authors say that broken homes "may also account for some of the differences between Negro and white intelligence scores." [43]

The scores of fifth graders with fathers absent were lower than the scores of first graders with fathers absent, and while the authors point out that it is cross sectional data and does not reveal the duration of the fathers' absence, "What we might be tapping is the cumulative effect of fatherless years." [44]

This difference in ability to perform has its counterpart in statistics on actual school performance. Nonwhite boys from families with both parents present are more likely to be going to school than boys with only one parent present, and enrollment rates are even lower when neither parent is present.

When the boys from broken homes are in school, they do not do as well as the boys from whole families. Grade retardation is higher when only one parent is present, and highest when neither parent is present.

The loneliness of the Negro youth in making fundamental decisions about education is shown in a 1959 study of Negro and white dropouts in Connecticut high schools.

Only 29 percent of the Negro male dropouts discussed their decision to drop out of school with their fathers, compared with 65 percent of the white males (38 percent of the Negro males were from broken homes). In fact, 26 percent of the Negro males did not discuss this major decision in their lives with anyone at all, compared with only 8 percent of white males.

A study of Negro apprenticeship by the New York State Commission Against Discrimination in 1960 concluded:

Negro youth are seldom exposed to influences which can lead to apprenticeship. Negroes are not apt to have relatives, friends, or neighbors in skilled occupations. Nor are they likely to be in secondary schools where they receive encouragement and direction from alternate role models. Within the minority community, skilled Negro 'models' after whom the Negro youth might pattern himself are rare, while substitute sources which could provide the direction, encouragement, resources, and information needed to achieve skilled craft standing are nonexistent. [45]

**Percent of Nonwhite Males Enrolled in School Who are 1 or More Grades
Below Mode for Age, by Age Group and Presence of Parents, 1960**

Age group	Both parents present	One parent present	Neither parent present
7-9 years	7.5	7.7	9.6
10-13 years	23.8	25.8	30.6
14-15 years	34.0	36.3	40.9
16-17 years.........	37.6	40.9	44.1
18-19 years.........	60.6	65.9	46.1

Source: 1960 Census, *School Enrollment,* PC(2) 5A, table 3, p. 24.

Delinquency and Crime

The combined impact of poverty, failure, and isolation among Negro youth has had the predictable outcome in a disastrous delinquency and crime rate.

In a typical pattern of discrimination, Negro children in all public and private orphanages are a smaller proportion of all children than their proportion of the population although their needs are clearly greater.

On the other hand Negroes represent a third of all youth in training schools for juvenile delinquents.

**Children in Homes for Dependent
and Neglected Children, 1960**

	Number	Percent
White	64,807	88.4
Negro..........	6,140	8.4
Other races	2,359	3.2
All races	73,306	100.0

Source: 1960 Census, *Inmates of Institutions,*
PC (2) 3A, table 31, p. 44.

It is probable that at present, a majority of the crimes against the person, such as rape, murder, and aggravated assault are committed by Negroes. There is, of course, no absolute evidence; inference can only be made from arrest and prison population statistics. The data that follow unquestionably are biased against Negroes, who are arraigned much more casually than are whites, but it may be doubted that the bias is great enough to affect the general proportions.

Number of arrests in 1963

	White	Negro
Offences charged total ..	31,988	38,549
Murder and nonnegligent manslaughter	2,288	2,948
Forcible rape.........	4,402	3,935
Aggravated assault.....	25,298	31,666

Source: *Crime in the United States* (Federal
Bureau of Investigation, 1963) table 25,
p. 111.

Again on the urban frontier the ratio is worse: 3 out of every 5 arrests for these crimes were of Negroes.

In Chicago in 1963, three-quarters of the persons arrested for such crimes were Negro; in Detroit, the same proportions held.

In 1960, 37 percent of all persons in Federal and State prisons were Negro. In that year, 56 percent of the homicide and 57 percent of the assault offenders committed to State institutions were Negro.

	Number of city arrests in 1963[1]	
	White	Negro
Offenses charged total ..	24,805	35,520
Murder and nonnegligent manslaughter	1,662	2,593
Forcible rape	3,199	3,570
Aggravated assault	19,944	29,357

[1]In 2,892 cities with population over 2,500

Source: *Crime in the United States* (Federal Bureau of Investigation, 1963) table 31, p. 117.

The overwhelming number of offenses committed by Negroes are directed toward other Negroes: the cost of crime to the Negro community is a combination of that to the criminal and to the victim.

Some of the research on the effects of broken homes on delinquent behavior recently surveyed by Thomas F. Pettigrew in *A Profile of the Negro American* is summarized below, along with several other studies of the question.

Mary Diggs found that three-fourths—twice the expected ratio—of Philadelphia's Negro delinquents who came before the law during 1948 did not live with both their natural parents.[46]

In predicting juvenile crime, Eleanor and Sheldon Glueck also found that a higher proportion of delinquent than nondelinquent boys came from broken homes. They identified five critical factors in the home environment that made a difference in whether boys would become delinquents: discipline of boy by father, supervision of boy by mother, affection of father for boy, affection of mother for boy, and cohesiveness of family.

In 1952, when the New York City Youth Board set out to test the validity of these five factors as predictors of delinquency, a problem quickly emerged. The Glueck sample consisted of white boys of mainly Irish, Italian, Lithuanian, and English descent.

However, the Youth Board group was 44 percent Negro and 14 percent Puerto Rican, and the frequency of broken homes within these groups was out of proportion to the total number of delinquents in the population.[47]

> In the majority of these cases, the father was usually never in the home at all, absent for the major proportion of the boy's life, or was present only on occasion.

(The final prediction table was reduced to three factors: supervision of boy by mother, discipline of boy by mother, and family cohesiveness within what family, in fact, existed, but was, nonetheless, 85 percent accurate in predicting delinquents and 96 percent accurate in predicting nondelinquents.)

Researchers who have focussed upon the "good" boy in high delinquency neighborhoods noted that they typically come from exceptionally stable, intact families.[48]

Recent psychological research demonstrates the personality effects of being reared in a disorganized home without a father. One study showed that children from fatherless homes seek immediate gratification of their desires far more than children with fathers present.[49] Others revealed that children who hunger for immediate gratification are more prone to delinquency, along with other less social behavior.[50] Two psychologists, Pettigrew says, maintain that inability to delay gratification is a critical factor in immature, criminal, and neurotic behavior.[51]

Finally, Pettigrew discussed the evidence that a stable home is a crucial factor in counteracting the effects of racism upon Negro personality.

> A warm, supportive home can effectively compensate for many of the restrictions the Negro child faces outside of the ghetto; consequently, the type of home life a Negro enjoys as a child may be far more crucial for governing the influence

of segregation upon his personality than the form the segregation takes—legal or informal, Southern or Northern.[52]

A Yale University study of youth in the lowest socioeconomic class in New Haven in 1950 whose behavior was followed through their 18th year revealed that among the delinquents in the group, 38 percent came from broken homes, compared with 24 percent of nondelinquents.[53]

The President's Task Force on Manpower Conservation in 1963 found that of young men rejected for the draft for failure to pass the mental tests, 42 percent of those with a court record came from broken homes, compared with 30 percent of those without a court record. Half of all the nonwhite rejectees in the study with a court record came from broken homes.

An examination of the family background of 44,448 delinquency cases in Philadelphia between 1949 and 1954 documents the frequency of broken homes among delinquents. Sixty-two percent of the Negro delinquents and 36 percent of white delinquents were not living with both parents. In 1950, 33 percent of nonwhite children and 7 percent of white children in Philadelphia were living in homes without both parents. Repeaters were even more likely to be from broken homes than first offenders.[54]

The Armed Forces

The ultimate mark of inadequate preparation for life is the failure rate on the Armed Forces mental test. The Armed Forces Qualification Test is not quite a mental test, nor yet an education test. It is a test of ability to perform at an acceptable level of competence. It roughly measures ability that ought to be found in an average 7th or 8th grade student. A grown young man who cannot pass this test is in trouble.

Fifty-six percent of Negroes fail it.

This is a rate almost four times that of the whites.

The Army, Navy, Air Force, and Marines conduct by far the largest and most important education and training activities of the Federal Government, as well as provide the largest single source of employment in the nation.

Juvenile Delinquents—Philadelphia by presence of parents, 1949-54

	White			Negro		
	All Court cases	First Offenders	Recidivists	All court cases	First Offenders	Recidivists
Number of Cases	20,691	13,220	4,612	22,695	11,442	6,641
Number not living with both parents	7,422	4,125	2,047	13,980	6,586	4,298
Percent not living with both parents	35.9	31.2	44.4	61.6	57.6	64.7

Source: Adapted from table 1, p. 255, "Family Status and the Delinquent Child," Thomas P. Monahan, *Social Forces*, March 1957.

ALMOST FOUR TIMES AS MANY NEGROES AS WHITES FAIL THE ARMED FORCES MENTAL TEST 1/

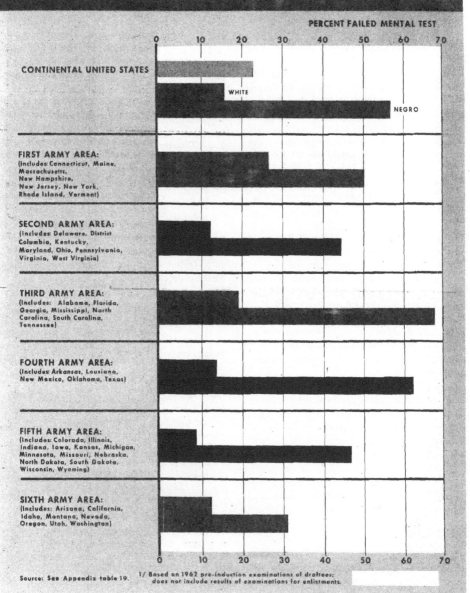

PERCENT FAILED MENTAL TEST

CONTINENTAL UNITED STATES
WHITE
NEGRO

FIRST ARMY AREA:
(Includes: Connecticut, Maine, Massachusetts, New Hampshire, New Jersey, New York, Rhode Island, Vermont)

SECOND ARMY AREA:
(Includes: Delaware, District Columbia, Kentucky, Maryland, Ohio, Pennsylvania, Virginia, West Virginia)

THIRD ARMY AREA:
(Includes: Alabama, Florida, Georgia, Mississippi, North Carolina, South Carolina, Tennessee)

FOURTH ARMY AREA:
(Includes: Arkansas, Lousiana, New Mexico, Oklahoma, Texas)

FIFTH ARMY AREA:
(Includes: Colorado, Illinois, Indiana, Iowa, Kansas, Michigan, Minnesota, Missouri, Nebraska, North Dakota, South Dakota, Wisconsin, Wyoming)

SIXTH ARMY AREA:
(Includes: Arizona, California, Idaho, Montana, Nevada, Oregon, Utah, Washington)

Source: See Appendix table 19.   1/ Based on 1962 pre-induction examinations of draftees; does not include results of examinations for enlistments.

- 41 -

Military service is disruptive in some respects. For those comparatively few who are killed or wounded in combat, or otherwise, the personal sacrifice is inestimable. But on balance service in the Armed Forces over the past quarter-century has worked greatly to the advantage of those involved. The training and experience of military duty itself is unique; the advantages that have generally followed in the form of the G.I. Bill, mortgage guarantees, Federal life insurance, Civil Service preference, veterans hospitals, and veterans pensions are singular, to say the least.

Although service in the Armed Forces is at least nominally a duty of all male citizens coming of age, it is clear that the present system does not enable Negroes to serve in anything like their proportionate numbers. This is not a question of discrimination. Induction into the Armed Forces is based on a variety of objective tests and standards, but these tests nonetheless have the effect of keeping the number of Negroes disproportionately small.

In 1963 the United States Commission on Civil Rights reported that "A decade ago, Negroes constituted 8 percent of the Armed Forces. Today . . . they continue to constitute 8 percent of the Armed Forces."[55]

In 1964 Negroes constituted 11.8 percent of the population, but probably remain at 8 percent of the Armed Forces.

Enlisted Men:	Percent Negro
Army	12.2
Navy	5.2
Air Force	9.1
Marine Corps	7.6
Officers:	
Army	3.2
Navy	.2
Air Force	1.2
Marine Corps	.2

The significance of Negro under-representation in the Armed Forces is greater than might at first be supposed. If Negroes were represented in the same proportions in the military as they are in the population, they would number 300,000 plus. This would be over 100,000 more than at present (using 1964 strength figures). If the more than 100,000 unemployed Negro men were to have gone into the military the Negro male unemployment rate would have been 7.0 percent in 1964 instead of 9.1 percent.

In 1963 the Civil Rights Commission commented on the occupational aspect of military service for Negroes. "Negro enlisted men enjoy relatively better opportunities in the Armed Forces than in the civilian economy in every clerical, technical, and skilled field for which the data permit comparison."[56]

There is, however, an even more important issue involved in military service for Negroes. Service in the United States Armed Forces is the *only* experience open to the Negro American in which he is truly treated as an equal: not as a Negro equal to a white, but as one man equal to any other man in a world where the category "Negro" and "white" do not exist. If this is a statement of the ideal rather than reality, it is an ideal that is close to realization. In food, dress, housing, pay, work—the Negro in the Armed Forces *is* equal and is treated that way.

There is another special quality about military service for Negro men: it is an utterly masculine world. Given the strains of the disorganized and matrifocal family life in which so many Negro youth come of age, the Armed Forces are a dramatic and desperately needed change: a world away from women, a world run by strong men of unquestioned authority, where discipline, if harsh, is nonetheless orderly and predictable, and where rewards, if limited, are granted on the basis of performance.

The theme of a current Army recruiting message states it as clearly as can be: "In the U.S. Army you get to know what it means to feel like a man."

At the recent Civil Rights Commission hearings in Mississippi a witness testified that his Army service was in fact "the only time I ever felt like a man."

Yet a majority of Negro youth (and probably three-quarters of Mississippi Negroes) fail the Selective Service education test and are rejected. Negro participation in the Armed Forces would be less than it is, were it not for a proportionally larger share of voluntary enlistments and reenlistments. (Thus 16.3 percent of Army sergeants are Negro.)

Alienation

The term alienation may by now have been used in too many ways to retain a clear meaning, but it will serve to sum up the equally numerous ways in which large numbers of Negro youth appear to be withdrawing from American society.

One startling way in which this occurs is that the men are just not there when the Census enumerator comes around.

According to Bureau of Census population estimates for 1963, there are only 87 nonwhite males for every 100 females in the 30-to-34-year age group. The ratio does not exceed 90 to 100 throughout the 25-to-44-year age bracket. In the urban Northeast, there are only 76 males per 100 females 20-to-24-years of age, and males as a percent of females are below 90 percent throughout all ages after 14.

There are not really fewer men than women in the 20-to-40 age bracket. What obviously is involved is an error in counting: the surveyors simply do not find the Negro

Ratio of Males per 100 Females in the Population, by Color, July 1, 1963

Age	Males per 100 Females	
	White	Nonwhite
Under 5	104.4	100.4
5-9 years	103.9	100.0
10-14 years	104.0	100.0
15-19 years.	103.2	99.5
20-24 years	101.2	95.1
25-29 years.	100.1	89.1
30-34 years	99.2	86.6
35-39 years.	97.5	86.8
40-44 years.	96.2	89.9
45-49 years.	96.5	90.6

Source: *Current Population Reports*, Series P-25, No. 276, table 1, (Total Population Including Armed Forces Abroad)

man. Donald J. Bogue and his associates, who have studied the Federal count of the Negro man, place the error as high as 19.8 percent at age 28; a typical error of around 15 percent is estimated from age 19 through 43.[57] Preliminary research in the Bureau of the Census on the 1960 enumeration has resulted in similar conclusions, although not necessarily the same estimates of the extent of the error. The Negro male *can* be found at age 17 and 18. On the basis of birth records and mortality records, the conclusion must be that he is there at age 19 as well.

When the enumerators do find him, his answers to the standard questions asked in the monthly unemployment survey often result in counting him as "not in the labor force." In other words, Negro male unemployment may in truth be somewhat greater than reported.

The labor force participation rates of nonwhite men have been falling since the beginning of the century and for the past decade have been lower than the rates for white men. In 1964, the participation rates were 78.0 percent for white men and 75.8 percent for nonwhite men. Almost one percentage point of this difference was due to a higher proportion of nonwhite men unable to work because of long-term physical or mental illness; it seems reasonable to assume that the rest of the difference is due to discouragement about finding a job.

If nonwhite male labor force participation rates were as high as the white rates, there would have been 140,000 more nonwhite males in the labor force in 1964. If we further assume that the 140,000 would have been unemployed, the unemployment rate for nonwhite men would have been 11.5 percent instead of the recorded rate of 9 percent, and the ratio between the nonwhite rate and the white rate would have jumped from 2:1 to 2.4:1.

Understated or not, the official unemployment rates for Negroes are almost unbelievable.

The unemployment statistics for Negro teenagers—29 percent in January 1965—reflect lack of training and opportunity in the greatest measure, but it may not be doubted that they also reflect a certain failure of nerve.

"Are you looking for a job?" Secretary of Labor Wirtz asked a young man on a Harlem street corner. "Why?" was the reply.

Richard A. Cloward and Robert Ontell have commented on this withdrawal in a discussion of the Mobilization for Youth project on the lower East Side of New York.

What contemporary slum and minority youth probably lack that similar children in earlier periods possessed is not motivation but some minimal sense of competence.

We are plagued, in work with these youth, by what appears to be a low tolerance for frustration. They are not able to absorb setbacks. Minor irritants and rebuffs are magnified out of all proportion to reality. Perhaps they react as they do because they are not equal to the world that confronts them, and they know it. And it is the knowing that is devastating. Had the occupational structure remained intact, or had the education provided to them kept pace with occupational changes, the situation would be a different one. But it is not, and that is what we and they have to contend with.[58]

Narcotic addiction is a characteristic form of withdrawal. In 1963, Negroes made up 54 percent of the addict population of the United States. Although the Federal Bureau of Narcotics reports a decline in the Negro proportion of new addicts, HARYOU reports the addiction rate in central Harlem rose from 22.1 per 10,000 in 1955 to 40.4 in 1961.[59]

There is a larger fact about the alienation of Negro youth than the tangle of pathology described by these statistics. It is a fact particularly difficult to grasp by white persons who have in recent years shown increasing awareness of Negro problems.

The present generation of Negro youth growing up in the urban ghettos has probably less personal contact with the white world than any generation in the history of the Negro American.[60]

Until World War II it could be said that in general the Negro and white worlds lived, if not together, at least side by side. Certainly they did, and do, in the South.

Since World War II, however, the two worlds have drawn physically apart. The symbol of this development was the construction in the 1940's and 1950's of the vast white, middle- and lower-middle class suburbs around all of the Nation's cities. Increasingly the inner cities have been left to Negroes—who now share almost no community life with whites.

In turn, because of this new housing pattern—most of which has been financially assisted by the Federal government—it is probable that the American school system has become *more*, rather than less segregated in the past two decades.

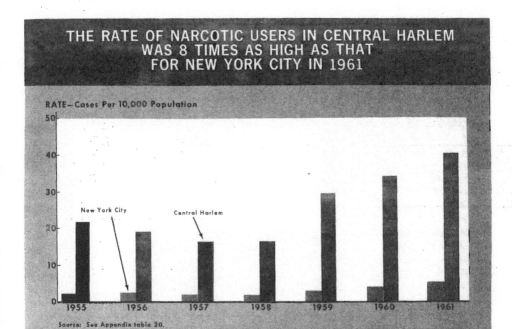

THE RATE OF NARCOTIC USERS IN CENTRAL HARLEM WAS 8 TIMES AS HIGH AS THAT FOR NEW YORK CITY IN 1961

RATE—Cases Per 10,000 Population

New York City

Central Harlem

Source: See Appendix table 20.

School integration has not occurred in the South, where a decade after *Brown v. Board of Education* only 1 Negro in 9 is attending school with white children.

And in the North, despite strenuous official efforts, neighborhoods and therefore schools are becoming more and more of one class and one color.

In New York City, in the school year 1957-58 there were 64 schools that were 90 percent of more Negro or Puerto Rican. Six years later there were 134 such schools.

Along with the diminution of white middle-class contacts for a large percentage of Negroes, observers report that the Negro churches have all but lost contact with men in the Northern cities as well. This may be a normal condition of urban life, but it is probably a changed condition for the Negro American and cannot be a socially desirable development.

The only religious movement that appears to have enlisted a considerable number of lower class Negro males in Northern cities of late is that of the Black Muslims: a movement based on total rejection of white society, even though it emulates whites more.

In a word: the tangle of pathology is tightening.

Chapter V

The Case For National Action

The object of this study has been to define a problem, rather than propose solutions to it. We have kept within these confines for three reasons.

First, there are many persons, within and without the Government, who do not feel the problem exists, at least in any serious degree. These persons feel that, with the legal obstacles to assimilation out of the way, matters will take care of themselves in the normal course of events. This is a fundamental issue, and requires a decision within the Government.

Second, it is our view that the problem is so inter-related, one thing with another, that any list of program proposals would necessarily be incomplete, and would distract attention from the main point of inter-relatedness. We have shown a clear relation between male employment, for example, and the number of welfare dependent children. Employment in turn reflects educational achievement, which depends in large part on family stability, which reflects employment. Where we should break into this cycle, and how, are the most difficult domestic questions facing the United States. We must first reach agreement on what the problem is, then we will know what questions must be answered.

Third, it is necessary to acknowledge the view, held by a number of responsible persons, that this problem may in fact be out of control. This is a view with which we emphatically and totally disagree, but the view must be acknowledged. The persistent rise in Negro educational achievement is probably the main trend that belies this thesis. On the other hand our study has produced some clear indications that the situation may indeed have begun to feed on itself. It may be noted, for example, that for most of the post-war period male Negro unemployment and the number of new AFDC cases rose and fell together as if connected by a chain from 1948 to 1962. The correlation between the two series of data was an astonishing .91. (This would mean that 83 percent of the rise and fall in AFDC cases can be statistically ascribed to the rise and fall in the unemployment rate.) In 1960, however, for the first time, unemployment declined, but the number of new AFDC cases rose. In 1963 this happened a second time. In 1964 a third. The possible implications of these and other data are serious enough that they, too, should be understood before program proposals are made.

However, the argument of this paper does lead to one central conclusion: Whatever the specific elements of a national effort designed to resolve this problem, those elements must be coordinated in terms of one general strategy.

What then is that problem? We feel the answer is clear enough. Three centuries of injustice have brought about deep-seated structural distortions in the life of the Negro American. At this point, the present tangle of pathology is capable of perpetuating itself without assistance from the white world. The cycle can be broken only if these distortions are set right.

In a word, a national effort towards the problems of Negro Americans must be directed towards the question of family structure. The object should be to strengthen the Negro family so as to enable it to raise and support its members as do other families. After that, how this group of Americans chooses to run its affairs, take advantage of its opportunities, or fail to do so, is none of the nation's business.

The fundamental importance and urgency of restoring the Negro American Family structure has been evident for some time. E. Franklin Frazier put it most succinctly in 1950:

As the result of family disorganization a large proportion of Negro children and youth have not undergone the socialization which only the family can provide. The disorganized families have failed to provide for their emotional needs and have not provided the discipline and habits which are necessary for personality development. Because the disorganized family has failed in its function as a socializing agency, it has handicapped the children in their relations to the institutions in the community. Moreover, family disorganization has been partially responsible for a large amount of juvenile delinquency and adult crime among Negroes. Since the widespread family disorganization among Negroes has resulted from the failure of the father to play the role in family life required by American society, the mitigation of this problem must await those changes in the Negro and American society which will enable the Negro father to play the role required of him. [61]

Nothing was done in response to Frazier's argument. Matters were left to take care of themselves, and as matters will, grew worse not better. The problem is now more serious, the obstacles greater. There is, however, a profound change for the better in one respect. The President has committed the nation to an all out effort to eliminate poverty where-ever it exists, among whites or Negroes, and a militant, organized, and responsible Negro movement exists to join in that effort.

Such a national effort could be stated thus:

The policy of the United States is to bring the Negro American to full and equal sharing in the responsibilities and rewards of citizenship. To this end, the programs of the Federal government bearing on this objective shall be designed to have the effect, directly or indirectly, of enhancing the stability and resources of the Negro American family.

FOOTNOTE REFERENCES

1. Robert Harris, *The Quest for Equality*, (Baton Rouge, Louisiana State University Press, 1960), p. 4.

2. William Faulkner, in a speech before the Southern Historical Society in November 1955, quoted in *Mississippi: The Closed Society*, by James W. Silver, (New York, Harcourt, Brace and World, Inc., 1964), p. xiii.

3. For a view that present Negro demands go beyond this traditional position see Nathan Glazer, "Negroes and Jews: The Challenge to Pluralism," *Commentary*, December 1964, pp. 29-34.

4. Bayard Rustin, "From Protest to Politics: The Future of the Civil Rights Movement," *Commentary*, February 1965, p. 27.

5. Nathan Glazer, op. cit., p. 34.

6. *Youth in the Ghetto*, Harlem Youth Opportunities Unlimited, Inc., New York, 1964, p. xi.

7. Nathan Glazer and Daniel Patrick Moynihan, *Beyond the Melting Pot*, (MIT Press and Harvard University Press, Cambridge, 1963), pp. 290-291.

8. E. Franklin Frazier, *Black Bourgeoisie*, (New York, Collier Books, 1962).

9. Furnished by Dr. Margaret Bright, in a communication on January 20, 1965.

10. Maurine McKeany, *The Absent Father and Public Policy in the Program of Aid to Dependent Children*, (Berkeley, University of California Press, 1960), p. 3.

11. "Facts, Fallacies and Future: A Study of the Aid to Dependent Children of Cook County, Illinois," (New York, Greenleigh Associates, Inc., 1960), p. 5.

12. Nathan Glazer, "Introduction," *Slavery*, Stanley M. Elkins, (New York, Grosset and Dunlap, 1963), p. ix.

13. Ibid., pp. xi-xii.

14. Ibid., pp. ix-x.

15. Thomas F. Pettigrew, *A Profile of the Negro American*, (Princeton, New Jersey, D. Van Nostrand Company, Inc., 1964), pp. 13-14.

16. Margaret Mead, *Male and Female*, (New York, New American Library, 1962), p. 146.

17. Ibid., p. 148.

18. E. Franklin Frazier, *The Negro Family in the United States*, (Chicago, The University of Chicago Press, 1939), p. 298.

19. Ibid., pp. 340-341.

20. Ibid., p. 487.

21. Edward Wight Bakke, *Citizens Without Work*, (New Haven, Yale University Press, 1940.)

22. Ibid., p. 212.

23. Ibid., p. 224.

24. Economic Report of the President, January 1965, p. 163.

25. Vera C. Perrella and Forrest A. Bogan, "Out of School Youth, February 1963," *Special Labor Force Report*, No. 46, Bureau of Labor Statistics, U. S. Department of Labor.

26. *Youth in the Ghetto*, op. cit., p. 185.

27. E. Franklin Frazier, *Black Bourgeoisie*, (New York, Collier Books, 1962.)

28. Robert O. Blood, Jr. and Donald M. Wolfe, *Husbands and Wives: The Dynamics of Married Living*, (Illinois, The Free Press of Glencoe, 1960), p. 34.

29. Ibid., p. 35.

30. Ibid.

31. Based on preliminary draft of a report by the President's Committee on Equal Employment Opportunity.

32. Whitney Young, *To Be Equal*, (New York, McGraw Hill Book Company, 1964), p. 25.

33. Ibid., p. 175.

34. Thomas F. Pettigrew, op. cit., p. 16.

35. Deton Brooks, quoted in *The New Improved American* by Bernard Asbell,(New York, McGraw Hill Book Company, 1965), p. 76.

36. Dorothy Height, in the Report of Consultation of Problems of Negro Women, President's Commission on the Status of Women, April 19, 1963, p. 35.

37. Duncan M.MacIntyre, *Public Assistance: Too Much or Too Little?* (New York, New York State School of Industrial Relations, Cornell University, Bulletin 53-1, December 1964), pp. 73-74.

38. Robin M. Williams, Jr., *Strangers Next Door*, (Englewood Cliffs, New Jersey, Prentice-Hall, Inc., 1964), p. 240.

39. *Youth in the Ghetto*, op. cit., p. 195.

40. Martin Deutch and Bert Brown, "Social Influences in Negro-White Intelligence Differences," *Social Issues*, April 1964, p. 27.

41. Ibid., p. 29.

42. Ibid.

43. Ibid., p. 31.

44. Ibid.

45. "Negroes in Apprenticeship, New York State," *Monthly Labor Review*, September 1960, p. 955.

46. Mary H. Diggs, "Some Problems and Needs of Negro Children as Revealed by Comparative Delinquency and Crime Statistics," *Journal of Negro Education*, 1950, 19, pp. 290-297.

47. Maude M.Craig and Thelma J. Glick,"Ten Years Experience with the Glueck Social Prediction Table," *Journal of Crime and Delinquency*, July 1963, p. 256.

48. F. R. Scarpitti, Ellen Murray, S. Dinitz and W. C. Reckless, "The 'Good' Boy in a High Delinquency Area: Four Years Later," *American Sociological Review*, 1960, 25, pp. 555-558.

49. W. Mischel, "Father-Absence and Delay of Gratification: Cross-Cultural Comparisons," *Journal of Abnormal and Social Psychology*, 1961, 63, pp. 116-124.

50. W. Mischel, "Preference for Delayed Reinforcement and Social Responsibility," *Journal of Social and Abnormal Psychology*, 1961, 62, pp. 1-7.
"Delay of Gratification, Need for Achievement, and Acquiescence in Another Culture," *Journal of Abnormal and Social Psychology*, 1961, 62, pp. 543-552.

51. O. H. Mowrer and A. D. Ullman, "Time as a Determinant in Integrative Learning," *Psychological Review*, 1945, 52, pp. 61-90.

52. Thomas F. Pettigrew, op. cit., p. 22.

53. Erdman Palmore, "Factors Associated with School Dropouts on Juvenile Delinquency Among Lower Class Children," *Social Security Bulletin*, October 1963, p. 6.

54. Thomas P. Monahan, "Family Status and the Delinquent Child," *Social Forces*, March 1957, p. 254.

55. Report of the U. S. Commission on Civil Rights, September 1963. p. 173.

56. Ibid., p. 174.

57. Donald J. Bogue, Bhaskar D. Misra, and D. P. Dandekar, "A New Estimate of the Negro Population and Negro Vital Rates in the United States, 1930-1960," *Demography*, Vol. 1, No. 1, 1964, p. 350.

58. Richard A. Cloward and Robert Ontell, "Our Illusions about Training," *American Child*, January 1965, p. 7.

59. *Youth in the Ghetto*, op. cit., p. 144.

60. Nathan Glazer and Daniel Patrick Moynihan, op. cit.

61. E. Franklin Frazier, "Problems and Needs of Negro Children and Youth Resulting from Family Disorganization," *Journal of Negro Education*, Summer 1950, pp. 276-277.

APPENDIX TABLES

1.... Percent of Nonwhite Married Women with Husbands Absent Due to Separation and Other Reasons, 1960.

2.... Percent of Married Women with Husbands Absent Due to Separation and Other Reasons, by Color, 1950-64.

3.... Estimated Number of Illegitimate Live Births and Ratio of Illegitimate Births to All Live Births, by Color, 1940-63.

4.... Rates of Illegitimate Births to All Live Births, Nonwhite, by City, 1950 and 1962.

5.... Families Headed by a Woman as Percent of all Families, by Color, Selected Periods, 1949-62.

6.... Percent Distribution of All Families by Type of Family, by Color, Selected Periods, 1949-62.

7.... Children on AFDC with Fathers Absent Compared with All Children on AFDC.

8.... Percent of Negro Families with Female Head, by Region and Area, 1960.

9.... Percent of White and Nonwhite Children Under 18 Not Living with Both Parents, United States, Urban and Rural, 1960.

10.... Unemployment Rates, by Color, U.S. and U.S. Excluding South, 1930-60.

11.... Percent of Nonwhite Married Women with Husbands Absent and Unemployment Rates of Nonwhite Males Aged 14 and Over.

12.... Percent of Nonwhite Married Women with Husbands Absent Compared with Unemployment Rates of Nonwhite Males Aged 14 and Over—Deviations From Linear Trend.

13.... Percent of Nonwhite Illegitimate Births in 1963 in District of Columbia Census Tracts as Related to Nonwhite 1960 Unemployment Rate of Census Tracts.

14.... Percent of Nonwhite Illegitimate Births in 1963 in District of Columbia Census Tracts as Related to Median Nonwhite Family Income in 1959 of Census Tracts.

15.... Extent of Unemployment Among Nonwhite Men, 1955-63.

16.... Fertility Rates, by Color, 1920-63 (Births per 1,000 Women, Age 15-44).

17.... Department of Labor Employment As Of December 31, 1964.

18.... Median IQ Scores for Central Harlem and New York City Pupils Compared to National Norms.

19.... The Rejection Rates for Failure to Pass the Armed Forces Mental Test, by Color.

20.... Habitual Narcotics Use—Cases and Rate per 10,000 Population for Central Harlem and New York City, 1955-61.

21.... Divorces, as Percent of Women Ever Married, United States, by Color, 1940 and 1947-64.

22.... Cases Opened Under AFDC (Excluding Unemployed Parent Segment) Compared With Unemployment Rate of Nonwhite Males.

Table 1

PERCENT OF NONWHITE MARRIED WOMEN WITH HUSBANDS ABSENT
DUE TO SEPARATION AND OTHER REASONS, 1960

City	Percent with Husband Absent due to Separation and Other Reasons	Percent Separated
Akron	16.1	11.9
Birmingham	18.5	13.8
Mobile	23.5	16.4
Denver	14.2	9.5
Hartford	25.7	19.9
Wilmington	23.9	17.3
Washington	23.5	16.1
Chicago	23.5	18.7
Detroit	19.2	14.9
St. Louis	23.1	18.5
New York City	30.2	21.5
Buffalo	22.3	17.7
Philadelphia	25.3	19.5
Pittsburgh	19.7	15.1
Baltimore	23.0	16.6
Houston	15.3	11.4
Dallas	17.2	11.8
San Antonio	16.1	9.0
Cleveland	18.5	14.1
Cincinnati	20.6	15.7
Milwaukee	18.2	13.5
Boston	23.5	15.9
New Orleans	22.2	15.7
Seattle	13.8	8.7
Memphis	22.6	17.7
Atlanta	22.6	16.8

Source: *U.S. Census of Population,* Vol. 1 —Selected States, table 105.

Table 2

PERCENT OF MARRIED WOMEN WITH HUSBANDS ABSENT DUE TO
SEPARATION AND OTHER REASONS, BY COLOR, 1950-64

Year	White		Nonwhite	
	Total[1]	Separated	Total[1]	Separated
1964	4.4	2.2	20.4	14.8
1963	4.4	1.9	21.2	14.6
1962	4.4	2.0	20.5	14.9
1961	4.3	2.2	19.6	14.3
1960	4.1	1.9	19.4	13.8
1959	4.4	1.8	23.3	17.6
1958	4.0	1.9	19.8	16.0
1957	4.2	1.7	17.9	13.1
1956	4.5	1.9	18.2	14.2
1955	5.3	2.3	21.9	15.1
1954	5.1	1.9	18.8	12.7
1953	4.7	1.8	15.7	10.6
1952	4.5	1.8	16.2	12.4
1951	n.a.	n.a.	16.1	12.1
1950	4.0	2.0	18.0	13.9

[1]Includes figures not shown separately.

Source: U.S. Bureau of the Census, *Current Population Series*, P-20.

Data for 1950 from 1950 Decennial Census because color break for
1950 is not available from *Current Population Survey*.

Table 3

ESTIMATED NUMBER OF ILLEGITIMATE LIVE BIRTHS
AND RATIO OF ILLEGITIMATE BIRTHS TO ALL LIVE BIRTHS
BY COLOR, 1940-63

Year	Number of Illegitimate Births (in thousands)			Illegitimacy Ratio [2]		
	Total	White	Nonwhite	Total	White	Nonwhite
1963[1]	259.4	102.2	150.7	63.3	30.7	235.9
1962	245.1	93.5	147.5	58.8	27.5	229.9
1961	240.2	91.1	149.1	56.3	25.3	223.4
1960	224.3	82.5	141.8	52.7	22.9	215.8
1959	220.6	79.6	141.1	52.0	22.1	218.0
1958	208.7	74.6	134.1	49.6	20.9	212.3
1957	201.7	70.8	130.9	47.4	19.6	206.7
1956	193.5	67.5	126.0	46.5	19.0	204.0
1955	183.3	64.2	119.2	45.3	18.6	202.4
1954	176.6	62.7	113.9	44.0	18.2	198.5
1953	160.8	56.6	104.2	41.2	16.9	191.1
1952	150.3	54.1	96.2	39.1	16.3	183.4
1951	146.5	52.6	93.9	39.1	16.3	182.8
1950	141.6	53.5	88.1	39.8	17.5	179.6
1949	133.2	53.5	79.7	37.4	17.3	167.5
1948	129.7	54.8	74.9	36.7	17.8	164.7
1947	131.9	60.5	71.5	35.7	18.5	168.0
1946	125.2	61.4	63.8	38.1	21.1	170.1
1945	117.4	56.4	60.9	42.9	23.6	179.3
1944	105.2	49.6	55.6	37.6	20.2	163.4
1943	98.1	42.8	55.4	33.4	16.5	162.8
1942	96.5	42.0	54.5	34.3	16.9	169.2
1941	95.7	41.9	53.8	38.1	19.0	174.5
1940	89.5	40.3	49.2	37.9	19.5	168.3

[1] Preliminary figures

[2] Per 1,000 total live births.

Source: U.S. Department of Health, Education, and Welfare; Public Health Service, National Vital Statistics Division; annual *Vital Statistics of the United States*.

Table 4

RATIO OF ILLEGITIMATE BIRTHS TO ALL LIVE BIRTHS, NONWHITE, BY CITY, 1950 AND 1962[1]

City	1950 Ratio	1962 Ratio	Percent Increase
Chicago.	222.9	289.9	30
Cincinnati	214.6	290.6	35
Cleveland	141.0	202.2	43
Dallas	187.2	252.4	35
Detroit	143.8	197.8	38
Houston.	160.8	272.9	70
Memphis	228.6	356.8	56
Milwaukee	153.5	203.2	32
Minneapolis	165.4	294.5	78
New Orleans	134.8	183.8	36
Philadelphia	223.9	233.3	4
Pittsburgh	191.5	208.1	9
St. Louis	237.8	292.3	23
San Antonio	100.5	157.8	57
Seattle	81.9	128.9	57
Washington, D. C. . . .	218.2	278.4	28

[1]Per 1,000 total live births.

Source: 1950 Rates: "Illegitimate Births: United States, 1938-57", U.S. Department of Health, Education and Welfare, 1963
1962 Rates: Computed from live birth and illegitimate birth statistics, *Vital Statistics of the U.S.* Volume I.

Table 5

FAMILIES HEADED BY A WOMAN AS PERCENT OF ALL FAMILIES BY COLOR, SELECTED PERIODS, 1949-62

Year	Families Headed by a Woman as Percent of Total	
	White	Nonwhite
1962.	8.6	23.2
1961.	8.9	21.6
1960.	8.7	22.4
1959.	8.4	23.6
1958.	8.6	22.4
1957.	8.9	21.9
1956.	8.8	20.5
1955.	9.0	20.7
1954.	8.3	19.2
1953.	8.4	18.1
1952.	9.2	17.9
1950.	8.4	19.1
1949.	8.8	18.8

Source: U.S. Department of Commerce, Bureau of the Census:
Current Population Reports, P-20, No. 125, 116, 106,
100, 88, 83, 75, 67, 53, 44, 33, and 26. Figures are
for March or April of each year.

Table 6

PERCENT DISTRIBUTION OF ALL FAMILIES BY TYPE OF FAMILY, BY COLOR, SELECTED PERIODS, 1949-62

Year	White				Nonwhite			
	All Families	Husband-Wife Families	Other Families With Male Head	Families With Female Head	All Families	Husband-Wife Families	Other Families With Male Head	Families With Female Head
1962	100.0	88.8	2.6	8.6	100.0	72.3	4.4	23.2
1961	100.0	88.6	2.5	9.0	100.0	74.4	3.9	21.6
1960	100.0	88.7	2.6	8.7	100.0	73.6	4.0	22.4
1959	100.0	88.8	2.8	8.4	100.0	72.0	4.4	23.6
1958	100.0	88.6	2.8	8.6	100.0	73.4	4.2	22.4
1957	100.0	88.4	2.8	8.9	100.0	74.7	3.4	21.9
1956	100.0	87.9	3.3	8.8	100.0	76.1	3.4	20.5
1955	100.0	87.9	3.0	9.0	100.0	75.3	4.0	20.7
1954	100.0	88.5	3.2	8.3	100.0	77.0	3.8	19.2
1953	100.0	88.2	3.4	8.4	100.0	78.6	3.4	18.1
1952	100.0	87.8	3.0	9.2	100.0	78.8	3.6	17.9
1950	100.0	88.4	3.1	8.4	100.0	76.8	4.3	19.1
1949	100.0	88.0	3.3	8.8	100.0	76.8	4.1	18.8

NOTE: Because of rounding, sums of individual items may not equal 100.

Source: U.S. Department of Commerce, Bureau of the Census: *Current Population Reports*, P-20, Nos. 125, 116, 106, 100, 88, 83, 75, 67, 53, 44, 33, and 26. Figures are for March or April of each year.

Table 7

CHILDREN ON AFDC WITH FATHERS ABSENT
COMPARED WITH ALL CHILDREN ON AFDC

Year	Total Children on AFDC	Children on AFDC Father Absent [1]	Percent
1963	2,952,000	1,889,000	64.0
1962	2,849,000	1,803,000	63.3
1961	2,613,000	1,666,000	63.8
1960	2,330,000	1,498,000	64.3
1959	2,247,000	1,404,000	62.5
1958	2,092,000	1,280,000	61.2
1957	1,832,000	1,104,000	60.3
1956	1,708,000	1,016,000	59.5
1955	1,692,000	983,000	58.1
1954	1,567,000	885,000	56.5
1953	1,494,000	820,000	54.9
1952	1,528,000	809,000	52.9
1951	1,618,000	827,000	51.1
1950	1,660,000	818,000	49.3
1949	1,366,000	648,000	47.4
1948	1,146,000	522,000	45.5
1947	1,009,000	441,000	43.7
1946	799,000	334,000	41.8
1945	647,000	257,000	39.7
1944	651,000	247,000	37.9
1943	746,000	269,000	36.1
1942	952,000	325,000	34.1
1941	946,000	304,000	32.1
1940	835,000	253,000	30.3

[1] Excludes those whose father was dead or incapacitated.

Source: *Trend Report*, "Graphic Presentation of Public Assistance and Related Data", HEW, 1963.

Table 8

PERCENT OF NEGRO FAMILIES WITH FEMALE HEAD, BY REGION AND AREA, 1960

Region	Urban	Rural Nonfarm	Rural Farm
United States.	23.1	19.5	11.1
Northeast	24.2	14.1	4.3
North Central	20.8	14.7	8.4
South	24.2	20.0	11.2
West.	20.7	9.4	5.5

Source: *U.S. Census of Population, 1960, Nonwhite Population by Race*, PC (2) 1C, table 9, pp 9-10.

Table 9

PERCENT OF WHITE AND NONWHITE CHILDREN UNDER 18 NOT LIVING
WITH BOTH PARENTS, UNITED STATES, URBAN AND RURAL, 1960

Area	Children Under 18 Without Both Parents	
	White	Nonwhite
United States	10.0	33.7
Urban................................	10.3	35.1
Rural Nonfarm	10.1	32.7
Rural Farm..........................	6.6	26.5

Source: *U.S. Census of Population, 1960, Social and Economic Characteristics* PC (1)-
1(C), table 79, p. 210.

Table 10

UNEMPLOYMENT RATES, BY COLOR, U.S. AND U.S. EXCLUDING SOUTH, 1930-1960

Color and Area	1960	1950	1940	1930[1]
United States				
White	4.7	4.5	14.2	6.6
Nonwhite	8.7	7.8	16.8	6.1
United States Excluding South				
White	4.8	4.9	14.8	7.4
Nonwhite	10.1	11.4	29.7	11.5

[1] Based in gainful worker concept. Includes persons 10 years of age and over.

Source: Bureau of Labor Statistics, computed from decennial censuses of population.

Table 11

**PERCENT OF NONWHITE MARRIED WOMEN WITH HUSBANDS
ABSENT AND UNEMPLOYMENT RATES OF NONWHITE
MALES AGED 14 AND OVER.**

Year	Percent of Nonwhite Married Women Separated from Their Husbands	Unemployment Rate for Nonwhite Males Aged 14 and Over
1963	14.6	10.6
1962	14.9	11.0
1961	14.3	12.9
1960	13.8	10.7
1959	17.6	11.5
1958	16.0	13.7
1957	13.1	8.4
1956	14.2	7.3
1955	15.1	8.2
1954	12.7	9.2
1953	10.6	4.4
1952	12.4	4.5
1951	12.1	4.4
1950		8.9
1949		8.8
1948		5.1

Source: Bureau of Labor Statistics, Department of Labor.

Table 12

PERCENT OF NONWHITE MARRIED WOMEN WITH HUSBANDS ABSENT COMPARED WITH UNEMPLOYMENT OF NONWHITE MALES AGED 14 AND OVER—DEVIATIONS FROM LINEAR TREND

Year	Percent of Nonwhite Married Women Separated from Their Husbands, Deviation from 1951-63 Linear Trend	Unemployment Rate for Nonwhite Males Aged 14 and Over, Deviation from 1948-62 Linear Trend
1963	-1.1	
1962	-0.5	-1.0
1961	-0.8	+1.4
1960	-1.0	-0.3
1959	+3.1	+0.9
1958	+1.8	+3.6
1957	-0.9	-1.2
1956	+0.5	-1.8
1955	+1.7	-0.4
1954	-0.4	+1.1
1953	-2.2	-3.2
1952	-0.1	-2.6
1951	-0.1	-2.2
1950		+2.7
1949		+3.1
1948		-0.1

Source: Bureau of Labor Statistics, Department of Labor.

Table 13

PERCENT OF NONWHITE ILLEGITIMATE BIRTHS IN 1963 IN DISTRICT OF COLUMBIA CENSUS TRACTS AS RELATED TO NONWHITE 1960 UNEMPLOYMENT RATE OF CENSUS TRACTS[1]

Census Tracts With Nonwhite Male Unemployment Rates of:—	Percent of Births Illegitimate
12.0 and over	40.8
9.0 -- 11.9	37.9
6.0 -- 8.9	31.1
3.0 -- 5.9	28.1
2.9 and below	17.6

[1]Census tracts with minority populations of 400 or more.

Source: Illegitimate Birth Statistics from D. C. Department of
Public Health; nonwhite male unemployment rates from
*Income, Education, and Unemployment in Neighborhoods,
Washington, D. C.* Bureau of Labor Statistics, Depart-
ment of Labor.

Table 14

PERCENT OF NONWHITE ILLEGITIMATE BIRTHS IN 1963 IN DISTRICT OF COLUMBIA CENSUS TRACTS AS RELATED TO MEDIAN NONWHITE FAMILY INCOME IN 1959 OF CENSUS TRACTS[1]

Census Tracts With Median Incomes of:—	Percent of Births Illegitimate
$8,000 and over.	12.0
$7,000 to $7,999	15.0
$6,000 to $6,999.	19.8
$5,000 to $5,999	24.8
$4,000 to $4,999	30.2
under $4,000	38.2

[1]Census tracts with minority populations of 400 or more.

Source: Illegitimate Birth Statistics from D. C. Department of Public Health; nonwhite family income from *Income, Education, and Unemployment in Neighborhoods, Washington, D. C.,* Bureau of Labor Statistics, Department of Labor.

Table 15

EXTENT OF UNEMPLOYMENT AMONG NONWHITE MEN, 1955-63

Year	All Unemployed as a Percent of Total Working or Looking for work	Unemployed who Worked During the Year as a Percent of Total Working	Percent of Unemployed who Worked During the Year Having Unemployment of 15 weeks or More
1963.....	29.2	27.0	48.5
1962.....	31.9	29.3	47.9
1961.....	34.1	31.6	48.2
1960.....	31.8	29.7	43.3
1959.....	27.8	26.0	NA
1958.....	31.6	29.1	NA
1957.....	NA	24.3	46.3
1956.....	NA	20.0	38.2
1955.....	NA	22.3	38.0

Source: Bureau of Labor Statistics, Department of Labor.

Table 16

FERTILITY RATES, BY COLOR, 1920-63
(Births per 1,000 Women, Age 15-44[1])

Year	White	Nonwhite	Year	White	Nonwhite
1963[2]	104.3	149.3	1941	80.7	105.4
1962	108.3	153.9	1940	77.1	102.4
1961	113.0	158.9	1939	74.8	100.1
1960	114.0	159.3	1938	76.5	100.5
1959	114.6	162.3	1937	74.4	99.4
1958	114.8	160.5	1936	73.3	95.9
1957	117.5	162.8	1935	74.5	98.4
1956	115.6	160.5	1934	75.8	100.4
1955	113.3	154.8	1933	73.7	97.3
1954	113.1	152.5	1932	79.0	103.0
1953	110.7	146.8	1931	82.4	102.1
1952	109.8	143.0	1930	87.1	105.9
1951	107.5	141.9	1929	87.3	106.1
1950	102.3	137.3	1928	91.7	111.0
1949	103.6	135.1	1927	97.1	121.7
1948	104.3	131.6	1926	99.2	130.3
1947	111.8	125.9	1925	103.3	134.0
1946	100.4	113.9	1924	107.8	135.6
1945	83.4	106.0	1923	108.0	130.5
1944	86.3	108.5	1922	108.8	130.8
1943	92.3	111.0	1921	117.2	140.8
1942	89.5	107.6	1920	115.4	137.5

[1]Adjusted for underregistration of births.
[2]Preliminary

Source: *Vital Statistics of the United States, 1962,* Volume I—Natality, table 1-2, pp. 1-4. The National Vital Statistics Division discontinued making adjustments for underregistration in 1959. Adjusted rates for 1960-1963 are based on estimates of underregistration supplied by the National Vital Statistics Division.

Table 17

DEPARTMENT OF LABOR EMPLOYMENT
AS OF DECEMBER 31, 1964

Grade	White[1]		Negro	
	Male	Female	Male	Female
Total	4,245	3,027	511	1,190
Average grade	11.26	6.29	6.81	4.84
Approximate Average salary	$9,240	$5,875	$6,800	$5,530
GS-18	7		1	
GS-17	23	2	1	
GS-16	38	3	3	
GS-15	261	21	3	
GS-14	408	53	9	1
GS-13	640	114	26	5
GS-12	877	147	36	13
GS-11	1,043	136	47	17
GS-10		9		
GS-9	448	210	59	40
GS-8	6	27	3	5
GS-7	221	282	55	82
GS-6	13	270	13	109
GS-5	104	757	70	350
GS-4	57	632	69	296
GS-3	84	313	78	238
GS-2	12	51	22	33
GS-1	3		16	1

[1] This is "Non-Negro" and may include some nonwhites other than Negro.

Source: Department of Labor.

Table 18

MEDIAN IQ SCORES FOR CENTRAL HARLEM AND NEW YORK CITY PUPILS COMPARED TO NATIONAL NORMS

Grade in School	Central Harlem	New York City	National
Third	90.6	98.6	100.0
Sixth	86.3	99.8	100.0
Eighth	87.7	100.0	100.0

Source: Harlem Youth Opportunities Unlimited, Inc., *Youth in the Ghetto,*
Adapted from chart 4, p. 193.

Table 19

REJECTION RATES FOR FAILURE TO PASS
THE ARMED FORCES MENTAL TEST, BY COLOR

	Number Examined, 1962	Failed Mental Test	
		Number	Percent
Continental United States	**286,152**	**64,536**	**22.6**
White	235,678	36,204	15.4
Negro	50,474	28,332	56.1
First Army Area:			
(Connecticut, Maine, Massachusetts, New Hampshire, New Jersey, New York, Rhode Island, Vermont)			
White	49,171	12,989	26.4
Negro	7,937	3,976	50.1
Second Army Area:			
(Delaware, District of Columbia, Kentucky, Maryland, Ohio, Pennsylvania, Virginia, West Virginia)			
White	48,641	5,888	12.1
Negro	9,563	4,255	44.5
Third Army Area:			
(Alabama, Florida, Georgia, Mississippi, North Carolina, South Carolina, Tennessee)			
White	30,242	5,786	19.1
Negro	20,343	13,772	67.7
Fourth Army Area:			
(Arkansas, Louisiana, New Mexico, Oklahoma, Texas)			
White	15,048	2,039	13.5
Negro	4,796	2,988	62.3
Fifth Army Area:			
(Colorado, Illinois, Indiana, Iowa, Kansas, Michigan, Minnesota, Missouri, Nebraska, North Dakota, South Dakota, Wisconsin, Wyoming)			
White	51,117	4,495	8.9
Negro	5,723	2,684	46.9
Sixth Army Area:			
(Arizona, California, Idaho, Montana, Nevada, Oregon, Utah, Washington)			
White	41,459	5,007	12.1
Negro	2,112	657	31.1

Source: Department of Defense, 1962. Examinations for the draft; does not include examination of applicants for enlistment.

Table 20

HABITUAL NARCOTICS USE – CASES AND RATE PER 10,000 POPULATION FOR CENTRAL HARLEM AND NEW YORK CITY, 1955-61

Year	Central Harlem		New York City	
	Cases	Rate[1]	Cases	Rate[1]
1961.........	934	40.4	4,006	5.2
1960.........	798	34.3	3,054	3.9
1959.........	693	29.5	2,413	3.1
1958.........	396	16.7	1,637	2.1
1957.........	395	16.5	1,654	2.1
1956.........	449	18.6	1,835	2.4
1955.........	542	22.1	1,828	2.3

[1]Per 10,000 population.

Source: Harlem Youth Opportunities Unlimited, Inc., *Youth in the Ghetto*, p. 144
(Based on data from New York City Department of Health, Bureau of
Preventable Diseases).

Table 21

DIVORCES, AS PERCENT OF WOMEN EVER MARRIED, UNITED STATES, BY COLOR, 1940 AND 1947-64

Year	Total	White	Nonwhite
1940	2.2	2.2	2.2
1947	2.7	2.6	3.1
1948	2.8	n.a.	n.a.
1949	2.8	n.a.	n.a.
1950	3.0[1]	3.0[1]	3.5[1]
1950	2.7	n.a.	n.a.
1951	2.6	n.a.	3.1
1952	2.8	2.7	3.5
1953	2.8	2.7	3.8
1954	2.8	2.7	3.9
1955	2.8	2.7	3.2
1956	3.0	2.9	4.0
1957	2.8	2.7	3.8
1958	2.9	2.8	3.5
1959	3.0	2.9	4.0
1960	3.3	3.0	5.4
1961	3.5	3.3	4.8
1962	3.3	3.1	5.0
1963	3.5	3.3	5.5
1964	3.8	3.6	5.1

[1]Data for 1950 from 1950 Decennial Census because color break for 1950 is not available from *Current Population Survey*; CPS total figure is 2.7 percent for 1950, so the same approximate difference can be assumed for white and nonwhite percents.

Source: U.S. Bureau of the Census, *Current Population Series*, P-20.

Table 22

CASES OPENED UNDER AFDC (EXCLUDING UNEMPLOYED PARENT SEGMENT) COMPARED WITH UNEMPLOYMENT RATE OF NONWHITE MALES

Year	AFDC Cases Opened [1]	Nonwhite Male Unemployment Rate
1964	429,048	9.1
1963	380,985	10.6
1962	370,008	11.0
1961	391,238	12.9
1960	338,730	10.7
1959	329,815	11.5
1958	345,950	13.7
1957	294,032	8.4
1956	261,663	7.3
1955	256,881	8.2
1954	275,054	9.2
1953	222,498	4.4
1952	234,074	4.5
1951	225,957	4.4
1950	291,273	8.9
1949	278,252	8.8
1948	210,193	5.1

[1] Does not include cases opened under program which commenced in some States in 1961 of assistance to children whose fathers are present but unemployed. There were 70,846 such cases opened in 1961, 81,192 in 1962, 80,728 in 1963, and 105,094 in 1964.

Source: AFDC cases opened from HEW; nonwhite male unemployment rates from Department of Labor.

U. S. GOVERNMENT PRINTING OFFICE : 1965 O

For sale by the Superintendent of Documents, U.S. Government Printing Office
Washington, D.C., 20402 - Price 45 cents

COSIMO is a specialty publisher of books and publications that inspire, inform, and engage readers. Our mission is to offer unique books to niche audiences around the world.

COSIMO BOOKS publishes books and publications for innovative authors, nonprofit organizations, and businesses. **COSIMO BOOKS** specializes in bringing books back into print, publishing new books quickly and effectively, and making these publications available to readers around the world.

COSIMO CLASSICS offers a collection of distinctive titles by the great authors and thinkers throughout the ages. At **COSIMO CLASSICS** timeless works find new life as affordable books, covering a variety of subjects including: Business, Economics, History, Personal Development, Philosophy, Religion & Spirituality, and much more!

COSIMO REPORTS publishes public reports that affect your world, from global trends to the economy, and from health to geopolitics.

FOR MORE INFORMATION CONTACT US AT
INFO@COSIMOBOOKS.COM

➤ if you are a book lover interested in our current catalog of books

➤ if you represent a bookstore, book club, or anyone else interested in special discounts for bulk purchases

➤ if you are an author who wants to get published

➤ if you represent an organization or business seeking to publish books and other publications for your members, donors, or customers.

**COSIMO BOOKS ARE ALWAYS
AVAILABLE AT ONLINE BOOKSTORES**

VISIT COSIMOBOOKS.COM
BE INSPIRED, BE INFORMED

CPSIA information can be obtained
at www.ICGtesting.com
Printed in the USA
BVHW060526241221
624768BV00009B/667